NOW GO LEAD YOURSELF

LEVEL UP YOUR LEADERSHIP IN 5 MINUTES A DAY

by Brandon Pinkerton

Now Go Lead Yourself by Brandon Pinkerton
Published by Now Go Lead

www.NowGoLead.com

Editing by Erica Ord and Angie Baker. Book Design, Layout and Cover by
Micah Bland, Elizabeth Kirkendall and Raylee Knight. Design and editing
at The Belford Group.

ISBN: 979-8-9935604-1-0

For information about special discounts available for bulk purchases,
sales promotions, fundraising and educational needs, contact Brandon
Pinkerton at
Sales@NowGoLead.com

This book is dedicated to all the leaders out there who are ready to start their own journey.

CONTENTS

ACKNOWLEDGEMENTS

My leadership journey started so long ago that I must thank the early influences in my life. My parents, who sacrificed so much to raise me well; Pat O'Brien, who encouraged me to grow in faith as a teen; Joe Taylor and Lynn Lloyd, who strongly influenced my college years. All of you generously shared your time and wisdom with me freely.

I must thank my business partner and best friend, Bill Hodge. It will always be a little profound to me that you would have the courage to take a chance on a young kid like me and start a business. We've been through a lot, brother, and I couldn't imagine taking a different path than the one we have walked together.

Had it been solely up to me and my own ambitions, this book would not exist. I am grateful to my Chief Human Resource Officer who collected much of the early office memos and emails that would become the foundations for this book. Thank you, MC!

Much thanks to my executive partners, Steve Williams and David Adams, who have supported me through the most challenging times in our business and continued to stay by my side through thick and thin. I hold our friendship in the highest regard.

I am grateful to every employee at HP Engineering, past and present, who has chosen to share their talents with me over the years. The life we have shared has been and continues to be such a deep source of inspiration for my leadership and writing. I will always be humbled by your decision to invest part of your life in following my lead.

Thanks to KD and TH, who helped me launch Now Go Lead (NGL) and collaborated with me on top of their normal workload. You were both a huge source of encouragement when I wanted to give up. KD, you are a rock star! Your vision for what NGL could be was much greater than my own. Your limitless bandwidth is a superpower beyond my reach.

Thanks to The Belford Group for making this project a tangible reality.

Thanks to my sister Brittney, who always answers the phone when I call her (sometimes daily). You have listened much more than you have spoken over the years. You are my biggest fan, and I appreciate you more than I can express.

Thanks to my three kids who have given me the opportunity to be a dad. Because of you I am reminded that true leadership starts in the home. I hope I am leading you well.

A very special thanks goes to my wife and true love, Camille; I know I am a handful most of the time. Your unwavering support has held me together in moments when I was ready to fall apart. In so many ways, you have given your life so I could pursue my vision, and I am endlessly blessed to have you by my side.

Finally, thanks to Father God, from whom all blessings flow. You are the True Rock and Source; the model of everything I am chasing on this journey. I hope I am making You proud.

THE INVITATION TO LEAD

Are you ready for this?

There is something equally exciting and unknown about an invitation. It is a generous gesture, a sign that someone, somewhere, wants you to join them and share an experience. The invitation to lead is like no other. You cannot yet know the joy and pain that you will encounter along your leadership journey. If you are fortunate, someone may walk beside you along the way. Although I can't physically accompany you on your individual path, know that I am with you in spirit as you embark on one of life's boldest endeavors—the pursuit of leadership.

My leadership philosophy has been shaped by my roots, my faith, and the experiences that are unique to my own journey—founding and growing my own business for the past twenty years. I grew up in a Christian home in rural Oklahoma. In my formative years, I was immersed in stories from the Bible, and so, I continue to draw deeply from this well to this day. There is a familiar story recorded in Exodus and made famous in the Hollywood film *The Ten Commandments*. After the Hebrews leave Egypt, Moses is called into a private meeting where God gives him the laws that will govern this emerging nation. But when Moses returns to share this revelation, he finds chaos—the people have lost focus and are "running wild." It is in this moment of failure and disorder God gives Moses this simple yet powerful mandate: "Now go, lead the people."

And so, from there, we have our invitation to go and lead. You may feel like things are in chaos right now, or you may simply be taking the budding steps towards your future destination. Whatever the case, where you go from here is largely up to you. I hope these writings and thoughts will be at times comforting and at others supremely challenging as you continue forward on a path that few will dare travel.

NOW GO LEAD

PROLOGUE

It's really hard to remember who I was when I took the first step on this journey. But looking back on the past 25 years, I can see clearly how who I am today is simply a manifestation of the path I've taken. The journey has broken me, molded me, and hardened me. I'm tougher, softer, and wiser—yet more aware than ever that I have only dipped my toes into the vast and deep ocean of whatever wisdom may be.

Now Go Lead began in 2018, when I started sending occasional emails to my company with my thoughts on leadership. About five years later, some special people who saved these emails encouraged me to share them with a wider audience. At first, I was reluctant. But I've learned in life to pay attention to the instincts of the people you trust the most. This book exists because of their belief that the world still needs authentic, grounded leadership.

In many ways, I'm smack in the middle of my own journey. With 25 years behind me, I stand at a crossroads—able to see the long path that's brought me here, while the future remains as uncertain as ever. Perhaps when I reach the end of my own journey, I'll be able to look back on this book and see whether the lessons still hold true. My hope is that it serves as a trusted guide for those who follow in my footsteps, and a reminder to those farther along of the enduring principles that mark the journey of leadership.

True leadership demands a mastery of your heart, mind, and soul, and there doesn't always seem to be a rhyme or reason for the path we take. The mercurial nature of the journey is reflected in these writings. They may seem erratic from one day to the next, being drawn from the context of a moment of crisis or the deep crash of emotion that spills onto the pages. One day the words will seem as if they were written specifically for you in your current moment on the journey, and other days the words may ring hollow. But the wonderful thing about truth is that it will hit you in a fresh way every time you read it. You may choose to read through this book more quickly than intended, but you'll gain so much more if you pace yourself and give the daily reading some time to sit with you and reveal the underlying truths. Given time, space, and an open heart, I believe that these words will leap off the page and hit home in the heart of a true leader. Here's to hoping these words find their target...

NOW GO LEAD

ALIGNED LEADERSHIP

Are you in alignment?

Everything you do as a leader matters; all of it. You cannot separate who you are at work from who you are at home for the same reason. You don't cease to be a leader when you stop working for the day. I might even go so far as to say what you do away from the eyes of your followers matters more than what you do when they are watching. It's easy to think that leadership brings more privileges and freedom. In truth, the opposite is often the case — when you choose to lead, you also choose to give some of those up for the good of others.

Why do I say that? Well, that is because leaders are held to a higher standard. Fair or not, it is the price of admission. You may not ask for it, and at first, you may not even realize it. But when you choose to lead, you enter into an unspoken agreement: your followers look to you to uphold their values.

This agreement extends to all areas of your life. It applies not only what you do in the office or in front of your organization, but also to your words and actions in your private moments. If this alignment breaks down, you will begin to lose followers. Eventually, you will have no one left to lead.

You can't (or at least shouldn't) *say* or *do* whatever you want and expect to retain the mantle of leadership. To be fair, there are plenty of so-called leaders who do not follow this rule. I call these people abusers of power, bullies, and frauds. But it is not what I will call true leadership in these writings. Not to say there is no room for failure along the way. We are, after all, human. Despite our best efforts, we will occasionally fall short. What we must avoid is creating a delusion in our minds that what we do in private has no effect on our leadership in public. Alignment matters, because as leaders we have no integrity without it.

In first century Israel, many Jews suffered under the abusive rule of their religious leaders. They were quick to hold people accountable for the hundreds of rules listed in the Talmud, even though they considered themselves to be above reproach.

In a scathing indictment against their style of leadership, Jesus told the people not to follow their example, because "they say one thing and do something else." The people were being held to extremely high standards by their leaders, but they were given no practical model of how to meet these standards in their daily lives. Even further, the leaders had no real intentions of doing the very things they were asking of everyone else.

Alignment of values and actions becomes especially important as you begin to build trust relationships with your team. There will be moments when you must ask a lot from someone, sometimes more than many would consider reasonable. When those moments arrive, your followers will make a split-second judgment about whether you have earned the right to expect their agreement. Everything you have modeled in front of your organization — the way you treat people, the way you handle relationships, the way you carry responsibility — will shape how your team responds to you in difficult situations.

Have you been asking your team to do things you are unwilling to do yourself? Don't expect your people to be loyal if you are not a loyal friend, spouse, or parent at home. Don't expect your team to take on greater amounts of responsibility if you are continually running from responsibility in your personal or professional life.

Everyone struggles with alignment at some point. Ideologies exist because they represent the perfection we strive for, even if we never fully attain it. That doesn't mean your leadership philosophy isn't worth pursuing, and it doesn't mean you should lower your standards. What it does mean is there is a profound need for leaders who set the bar high for themselves and choose each day to reach for that goal.

NOW GO LEAD

FIVE MINUTE REFLECTION

What's an area of your life that needs alignment with your leadership values? What will it take for you to level up your leadership by aligning your words and actions?

90 DAYS

Can 90 Days Really Change Anything?

Ask the question to anyone who has been a part of the hit show *90 Day Fiancé*, and the answer would be a resounding yes! The idea of a "90-day program" has become ubiquitous in many areas these days, whether it's evaluating a new employee's long-term job potential or trying out a diet or exercise program. The premise is simple: if you can commit to a behavior or routine for 90 days, you can have a pretty good idea of whether you will achieve long-term results by continuing the program.

So, I recently began wondering: What would happen if you intently focused on your leadership growth for 90 days? Could meaningful change happen in that amount of time?

The idea of growing your leadership in 90 days may seem abstract at first. But as with any other endeavor, the most critical element is taking the first step. Everyone reading this is at a different place in their journey, which means the starting line is going to look a little different depending on how long you've been pursuing your own vision. The goal is to establish a baseline for where you are today and then set specific benchmarks to measure success over the next 90 days. To do this well, you'll need to set aside your pride, stay humble, and remain open to the idea that every one of us has room to grow.

"WHAT NEEDS TO CHANGE?"

A good starting point is to ask yourself a straightforward yet challenging question: *What needs to change?* This question will ultimately determine the trajectory of the next 90 days.

I'll forewarn you, though the answer may be uncomfortable. Depending on your courage to face it honestly, the challenge could be over before you ever take the first step.

REFLECTION

Take a moment to grab your journal. Write down the question and take about 20 minutes to search your soul for the answers. If you find yourself not coming up with much, the assessment below may help you clarify your baseline.

BASELINE LEADERSHIP ASSESSMENT

Rate each statement on a scale of 1 to 10, 1 being not true, 10 being very true.

1. I have made measurable progress towards my vision in the past year.
2. I know what I need to be working on every day to make progress.
3. I am disciplined with my time and not letting daily distractions slow me down.
4. I measure success using clear metrics instead of comparing myself to others.
5. I am honest with myself about my shortcomings and lead with humility.
6. I am aware of the personal biases that impact my leadership abilities.
7. My closest relationships are healthy.
8. I regularly have 1-on-1 time with a mentor.
9. I am mentoring at least 2-3 others in my organization regularly.
10. I am open and vulnerable in my important relationships.
11. I have open channels for receiving feedback from my team or organization.
12. I have a clear sense of who I am as a leader.

If you had trouble answering some of the questions above, it may be because the assessment assumes you already have a vision and are actively leading others. If this is not your current situation, it's okay. We need to start somewhere. There are a lot of great tools out there to help you set a vision for yourself or your organization, and that, in and of itself, would be a great 90-day goal for you. Whatever your starting point, you now have enough information to form a picture of what the next 90 days could look like for your leadership journey.

"WHAT NEEDS TO BE DONE?"

With your baseline in place, we can start considering the practical steps towards measurable progress. Take your two or three lowest-scoring personal assessment ratings and filter them again through the question: *What needs to change?* Now we need to think critically about what needs to be done to make improvements.

Let's walk through an example: I am disciplined with my time and not letting daily distractions slow me down (RATE 1-10): **3**

What needs to change?
> I need more focus.

What needs to be done?
> I need to remove some specific distractions from my life.
> I need greater discipline and accountability around my screen time.
> I need to address a relationship issue that is distracting my leadership.

The process is not complicated. The hard part is sticking to the plan. But imagine what could happen if you reclaimed even four hours a week currently lost to a distracting app or an unresolved relationship issue. That alone could dramatically increase your leadership capacity.

"HOW WILL I MEASURE SUCCESS?"

With a plan in place, I recommend you get external accountability to help you stay on track and measure your success. Weekly check-ins with a trusted person or team can help you stay on track. Personally,

I'm a huge fan of Wickman's Traction tools, but any consistent account-ability system will work.

Continuing our example, let's say your goal for the next 90 days is to capture four (4) hours of leadership focus every week. The reality is, at first, you may not fully be aware of every distraction keeping you from the focus you need. Nevertheless, the most important step is to start.

What needs to change?
   I need more focus.

What needs to be done?
   I need to remove some specific distractions from my life.
   I need greater discipline and accountability around my screen time.
   I need to address a relationship issue that is distracting my leadership.

How will I measure success?
   I will track my ability to gain four hours of leadership focus each week.

	Week 1	Week 2	Week 3	Week 4
Target	4	4	4	4
Actual	2	4	3	4

Weekly to do(s):
   Add intentional focus time to my calendar
   Remove Facebook app from my phone

REFLECTION

As you track your weekly progress, note the behaviors or obstacles holding you back from meeting your goals. As these issues manifest, commit to addressing them before the next weekly check-in. After 90 days of small, intentional steps, you will see significant growth.

The final, and often overlooked, step in the 90 Day Challenge is to celebrate the gains. Of course, I'd love to hear your story myself (send an email to Brandon@NowGoLead.com). But even if you decide not to trumpet your success to the world, your accountability group will be a great place to share in your victory. I'm truly looking forward to watching your leadership improve in the next 90 days. It's time to embark on the next great stretch in your leadership journey!

NOW GO LEAD

FIVE MINUTE REFLECTION

Am I willing to commit the next 90 days of my journey to growing my leadership?
Write out a statement committing to grow your leadership over the next 90 days.

TRIALS AND TREASURES

How do I harness experience?

The leader is not immune to craving normalcy and a sense of routine. These desires intensify during times of crisis. Even the leader, who has their most heroic moments in times of great need, is grateful for seasons of trial to end so they can retreat to the comfort of routine.

I hear this sentiment from leaders in crisis all the time: "I just want things to get back to normal." I completely understand. Consider, though, there is something important to be learned in every trial; it's the treasure. The greatest tragedy is when a leader walks out of a crisis and immediately slips back into old patterns, leaving the treasure behind.

When I started my business, I quickly latched onto journaling as a way to capture lessons from failures and missed opportunities. There were so many of these moments early on that it was truly difficult to keep track of everything happening. We were prolific in our production, meeting deadlines, cranking out designs, but we were not taking any time to evaluate the quality of our work or the processes behind it.

Soon, customer complaints started flooding my inbox and voicemail. Lacking a better system, I grabbed a yellow legal pad and began writing down everything we needed to fix. I kept the legal pad right by my keyboard at all times. I'd read an angry email and then write a new rule. I'd navigate a difficult conversation with a customer and jot down what not to do next time.

Eventually the pages of the legal pad became the foundation for our first quality control process, and production improved dramatically.

Looking back, what started out as a product of desperation became a priceless treasure.

Often, when difficulty strikes your organization, you can clearly see what happened to lead you to your circumstances. What's harder is learning how to keep it from happening again. Sometimes it was your previous system that failed; other times, it was your lack of adherence to it. Ask yourself: What needs to change? If you return to the old routines without adjustment, you're setting yourself up for the same results.

The treasure is the reward: the learning, the wisdom, the new clarity, that, should you choose to take it with you, will grow. It's what matters most because it may be the only thing redeemable when tragedy hits hard. The leader must continually fight to capture the moment rather than wishing it away.

NOW GO LEAD

FIVE MINUTE REFLECTION

Are you in crisis? Reflect on what has brought you to this moment. Is your "normal" way of doing things consistently creating problems? Are you willing to look in the mirror and honestly acknowledge what needs to change?
What is the treasure you can find hidden inside of this trial?

IMITATION

Am I Worth Imitating?

Mimicry often gets a bad rap in our culture. We're encouraged to "stand apart" and "be yourself." Those can be good things, but sometimes they give people license to behave however, they want without considering the consequences. The attitude becomes, "Hey, I'm just being me."

Leadership calls you to something higher than simply managing people. As I've mentioned before, when you choose to become a leader, you also accept the sacrifices that come with that decision. What was once acceptable behavior when you had no followers will now fall under the scrutiny of your entire organization, and that's absolutely fair. Not only that, you must now intentionally develop leadership behaviors and make a plan to address the personal shortcomings capable of holding back organizational growth if left unaddressed.

As soon as you step into a leadership position, you'll start to struggle with the dynamics of teams building and organizational growth. One of the first challenges you'll encounter is getting the team to understand and follow the core values that will guide you along the journey. Holding your growing organization accountable to these behaviors can be a real challenge and your ability to lead well starts with the tone you set. This becomes especially challenging when you identify large gaps between a particular core value and your own leadership habits.

Take the common value of being proactive. You may want everyone to get their timesheets done weekly without a call from accounting. However, everyone on your team knows you never get your own timesheet done until the last minute, either. There are countless examples like this, but the principle is simple: what you **DO** speaks louder than what you **SAY**.

Over and over again on my own leadership journey, the pressure to grow did not come from an outside influence, a book, or a podcast. It came from my organization compelling me to be the kind of leader they wanted to follow and would be proud to have at the front of the line. For me, it started early with my physical appearance. I bought the best clothes I could afford responsibly. I took pride in looking like I belonged in the role, even while my experience was still catching up.

Later on, as we grew, another critical need emerged: supporting our employees' personal and career goals. I asked all leaders to start having regular 1-to-1 meetings with their teams. I nearly had a revolt on my hands because of this simple request.

"Brandon, how do you expect me to take an extra hour out of my day to meet with my people and talk about our feelings! I'm already talking to them every day. This seems like a real waste of everyone's time."

But I believed in the concept, and I knew I had no right to expect anyone to embrace it unless I modeled it myself. So, I began by setting regular recurring meetings with everyone on my team and fiercely protecting the time on my calendar. I also invested deeply in each meeting and made sure I was focused and prepared to make them meaningful. Eventually, our organization began to see value in these encounters as more than just a good idea. They saw the impact—and they followed my lead. Those meetings changed our culture.

Every eye is on you as a leader of your organization. Choosing to lead well means submitting who you are to what the organization needs you to be. Your people are looking for someone worth following — someone whose life offers an example to imitate. Be that example, and pursue the vision with commitment and integrity.

NOW GO LEAD

FIVE MINUTE REFLECTION

When emotions run high – Am I worth imitating?
When the crap hits the fan – Am I worth imitating?
When no one is looking – Am I worth imitating?
What are some things that need to change so that I am worth imitating?

BUT I'VE ALREADY COMMITTED SO MUCH!

Are you making progress toward the right goal?

Imagine you are a mountain climber who realizes halfway up you're ascending the wrong peak. Every step takes you closer to the top, but farther from your desired destination. You pause and consider: I've put so much work into getting to this point. *Can I really turn back now? What will people say? Will my followers lose confidence in me?*

It takes tremendous courage for a leader not to climb higher, but to descend, to acknowledge the misstep, pivot, and begin again on the right mountain. Pivoting is a critical leadership skill. Knowing *when* to pivot takes years of practice and often comes with a long list of lessons learned. It can be frustrating to pour yourself into an initiative only to realize you've chosen the wrong path. Believe me, I know.

During my first year of college, I got an unexpected phone call in my dorm room from a woman I had never met before. She worked for General Motors and asked if I was interested in a potential summer internship. I had no idea how she found me or why she was interested in me, but after a brief phone interview, I was offered a position at the Oklahoma City assembly plant for the summer. It felt like a providential moment in my life.

Over the next three summers, I continued taking on new internships in Detroit, and upon graduation, my new bride and I moved to Michigan to begin our new life together and build upon the career I had started.

Things moved quickly. I received a couple of quick promotions and was presented with a path for long-term success within the company. But something began stirring in me. The thought of spending my life 800 miles away from family didn't feel like the future I wanted.

A real crisis began forming. On the outside, I looked successful — the small-town kid who made it in the big city. On the inside, I was deeply unhappy, and the thought of quitting my job and starting over made me sick to my stomach. I had committed so much time and energy. Walking away felt like failure.

With my wife's full support, we decided to pivot and relocate back home. I think the hardest phone call was to my dad. For whatever reason, I was afraid he might admonish me for giving up, or maybe I was worried he just wouldn't be as proud of me. But instead of criticism, I received open arms and understanding from the people who were happy to have me back. I took a significant pay cut and started over in a new engineering field. It was tough. But looking back, it was a pivotal moment that ultimately led me to greater success in life.

CHANGING COURSE IS NOT REGRESSION

It takes an enormous amount of courage to pivot towards what truly matters. As leaders, we can fall into the trap of believing that moving forward in *any direction* is better than retreat. But as Stephen R. Covey says: "If the ladder is not leaning against the right wall, every step we take just gets us to the wrong place faster."

YOUR PAST DOES NOT DICTATE YOUR FUTURE

Leader, you must understand this: past decisions don't have to dictate your future. You'll make mistakes. You'll invest time, energy, and resources into failed initiatives, bad opportunities, and unhealthy relationships. You also have the freedom to make choices based on what lies ahead, not what lies behind.

You can't lead from fear of what other people might think about your decision. Every misstep is a lesson, not a loss. Shift your perspective from what was spent to what was learned. When you build the habit of reassessing your commitments and disengaging from the ones no longer serving your mission, you cut through indecision and make far greater progress toward what truly matters.

NOW GO LEAD

<u>FIVE MINUTE REFLECTION</u>

Are you making decisions based on past investments rather than future benefits?
What is a course of direction you've pursued that might need to change?

THE SOUL OF THE LEADER

What lives in the soul of the leader?

I have never met anyone who can conceal who they are all the time. Everyone likes to put on a good face, but eventually our true essence, or soul, will emerge.

One of the most challenging lessons I had to learn was how to identify potential next-generation leaders in our organization. When you ask people about leadership, many believe they want to be in charge, and it's not unusual for them to say the right words to create the image they want us to see. We've all done it at some point.

I remember trying to fill a leadership and management position for one of our regional offices. We had been struggling to fill the position for some time when we finally found someone who seemed perfect. We'll call him Nate.

Nate was well-credentialed with an advanced degree who said all the right things and gave me the warm fuzzies during our interview. I walked away feeling convinced that he was the right person to lead our regional office to long-term success. So, we offered him the job, and he accepted.

To be fair, Nate stepped into a difficult situation left behind by his predecessor, which meant he would have to take on some legacy issues. However, he was confident he could fix those issues. For the first year, things went pretty smoothly. But eventually, we reached a point where we could no longer blame the previous regime for some of the ongoing problems. That's when Nate's true leadership heart began to show. Instead of acknowledging his shortcomings, he blamed, deflected, and excused.

Nate knew a lot *about* leadership, and he used his knowledge to project an image that wasn't actually genuine. In the end, all the "good ideas" and leadership bravado collapsed because they weren't rooted in a true representation of his heart.

LEADING FROM THE HEART

Every leader faces moments when they feel tempted to lead from a place disconnected from their true self. You read something new, hear a fresh idea, or feel pressure from your organization to act like someone you're not. Don't fall into this trap!

A leader must consistently see the difference between growth-producing changes and those pulling them away from their heart. One grows your leadership; the other erodes your integrity. To successfully navigate this constant demand for change, the leader must stay self-aware and centered. Don't ever be afraid to stay on course. Don't chase every "latest trend." Leadership becomes far easier once you stop letting the clutter influence your heart.

Your story, the real one, is filled with victories, failures, pride, and regret. But it is also filled with resilience. Embrace your story and stay true to your soul. The story of your pursuit will also unfold in the lives of the people who trust your authentic leadership.

NOW GO LEAD

FIVE MINUTE REFLECTION

What am I allowing to speak to the soul of my leadership?
Is my leadership a true reflection of my convictions?
If not, then why not?
Have I potentially made compromises that are turning my eyes
away from the vision? How can I get my eyes back on the vision?

SHICERS

Are you afraid of being found out?

I was out on a walk recently when this question hit me: Does the way I live my life validate my message, or am I more likely to be exposed as a leadership fraud? We all say a lot of things. We talk a big game. We make sure everyone sees our best side. However, if you're secretly worried about being exposed as a fraud, you may feel tempted to play it safe — to challenge others only in areas you feel completely confident in managing yourself. But that isn't leadership; it's called sandbagging.

When I've shared this "fear of being found out" with others, I often get corrected or gently reminded to be more confident in my leadership abilities. I think people respond this way because they assume I'm wrestling with paralyzing doubts, which is not the case. In truth, this "fear of being found out" is a powerful motivator for me, a reminder to live above reproach and protect my integrity. I believe this is healthy.

What I've learned over the years is that our brains are actually wired to respond to this kind of tension. Neuroscience tells us that when we feel a hint of risk or uncertainty, the amygdala wakes up and signals the rest of the brain to focus. Chemicals like dopamine and norepinephrine get released, sharpening our attention and pushing us to rise to the moment. It's why a little pressure can bring out our best, while a life with no challenge slowly lulls us into complacency.

I find this fascinating because it means the "fear of being found out" isn't always a flaw. Sometimes it's the very thing that keeps us honest, keeps us growing, and keeps us living in alignment with the message we're asking others to follow.

Real leadership happens when you're courageous enough to create a bold vision and inspire others to pursue it with you. The fake leader, on the other hand, presents an image of someone who has already "arrived" through powerful speeches, pretension, and even false modesty. The message becomes, "I've already figured this out, and I need you to get your life up to my level." I've watched many leaders like this inspire thousands, only to be undone by scandal or private failures. The truth is, they were never committed to their own vision and believed the standard applied only to others.

You may ask, "Isn't that asking a lot?" Of course it is. This path is only for those brave enough to commit their entire lives to the vision. Don't let complacency seep into your leadership by eliminating every trace of fear. Harness it and use it to strengthen your authenticity.

NOW GO LEAD

FIVE MINUTE REFLECTION

Am I afraid to set a powerful vision because I lack the commitment to follow through in my own life?
Have I set the limits on my leadership based on my comfort level?
How can I use my fear to propel me to act in a positive way?

METAMORPHOSIS

What are you becoming?

If I were to ask you what you want to be in five years or ten years, what would you tell me? Would it be a title like *vice-president* or *mom*? Or would it be more qualitative, like *wealthy* or *healthy*? Whatever the case, I genuinely hope you have a vision of what you want to become and the vision is much greater than your ability to understand how to make it happen. Along the leadership journey, you need to understand how the greater the change you are trying to achieve, the more you will have to give up your current circumstances and comforts.

I remember my early science lessons in elementary school about how a caterpillar becomes a butterfly. It is a simple concept used to teach young children that we all go through changes in our lives and even though we may not like who we are today, one day we will go through a process and become something, hopefully better. It wasn't until recently that I came across a scientific article explaining what we *do*, and more specifically, *don't* know about what happens when this creature spends time in the chrysalis phase of its existence. It's fascinating.

When I was growing up in the country, I remember coming home from school, looking for caterpillars and trying to guess what they would become one day. I would also try to reason out which parts of the caterpillar would become the eyes, wings, and legs of the butterfly. Of course, never being able to see inside the chrysalis, I had no idea what actually happened in there. What scientists now understand is when butterflies enter the chrysalis stage, they don't simply "grow wings;" they undergo an astonishing rebuild. Much of the caterpillar's body breaks down and gets recycled, while groups of specialized cells - present all along - begin building the adult butterfly's features in a tightly choreographed transformation. From the outside, it looks like stillness. Inside, it's an organized teardown and a deliberate re-creation into something genuinely different. As an engineer, it is mind-blowing to me. But as a leader, it resonated with me perfectly.

What if I told you that you could become the very thing you want to be, but the price would be a complete dissolution of your current state of being? Would you sign up for that? The problem is we are often too comfortable with our current life. We are accustomed to our ways, our circumstances, and habits. We might occasionally experience something painful that stirs us to action, but too often we just settle back to our normal workaday lives. The truth is: the caterpillar who never decides to undergo a radical change is doomed to die while they get fat under the safety of what's familiar. Though death is inevitable, only the butterfly knows the freedom of flying beyond the canopy of safety, tasting the breathtaking moments only found in the unbridled open air of the great expanse.

Another interesting thought is, even though they are effectively the same combination of biological material, the caterpillar cannot understand what it means to be a butterfly, nor can it even attempt the things a butterfly can do easily. In the same way, the butterfly loses all memories of its old life and can never return to its old way of life. It has become so fundamentally different - it has lost all ability to exist as it once was. Essentially, there is no going back.

Be warned - there is a great burden in learning what you want to become because every action going forward will either take you closer to or move you away from your vision. However, this knowledge can bring great clarity as to where you should spend your energy each day. Did your actions today take you closer or take you away from that goal? We make progress along the journey when we stop doing the things taking us away and do more of the things that bring us closer to greatness.

NOW GO LEAD

FIVE MINUTE REFLECTION

What is the plan for what I want to become?
Is it something big enough that I can't map the whole path yet, only the next step?
Am I willing, in an act of faith, to completely give up everything I am and all that I have to undergo the process of change?
Can I leave my comfortable life behind to pursue the highest levels of leadership?

OVERNIGHT SUCCESS

How long does it take?

Success, however you define it, is something we choose to pursue along the journey. Success is that often-moving goal representing the culmination of our dreams and aspirations. It is what comes to mind when we think about fulfillment and a meaningful existence. Life can almost be summarized as a series of years and seasons spent pursuing success. Whether we are working toward an education, building a career, or investing in a long-term relationship, most of what we do each day is aimed at one thing: becoming who we believe we are meant to be.

But then again, life is incredibly long. The idea of waiting years or decades to achieve success is unappealing, especially when the world would have us believe so many people are finding it more quickly than we are. The poisonous message social media has hammered into our brains is - success can be achieved quickly if we follow trends and make the best use of the latest shortcuts and life hacks. The way our modern brains are wired, we have begun to choose short-term happiness over success. Subsequently, we have developed this fear of missing out, which diverts us from the path of consistency that leads to lasting success.

While their paths have all been different, there is one thing in common for the most successful people in the world: consistency and patience. Warren Buffett gained the vast majority of his wealth after age 50, as did Elon Musk. Mark Zuckerberg turned down a billion dollars at age 22; he's now worth two hundred times that amount as he enters his 40s. Take a look at any generation still in the work force. You will see average job tenures are nowhere close to the decades it often takes to reach the stratosphere of the elites.

But you may say, "Hey, money isn't everything." Ok, let's take a look at relationships. The average marriage in the US lasts only 8 years, which means we aren't doing too much better there either. Very recently, scientists discovered close relationships as one of the leading indicators of a long life, even more than diet and exercise.

So yeah, money is important and so are relationships, but for whatever reason, we seem to be choosing short-term options to get ourselves out of difficult situations. It reveals a striking truth: Only a small percentage of people have the mental and emotional toughness to keep going when everyone else has run for the hills.

In a "do what's best for yourself" world, you will receive plenty of accolades and encouragement for doing what's best for you in the moment, and you will only get puzzled looks and maybe ridicule for staying with something during a season of uncertainty or discomfort.

Lasting success doesn't happen overnight. It is the result of an unnatural focus of mind and body built on the growth coming from staying firm in the storms that wipe out people, leaders, and organizations with shallow foundations and low resolve. I hope today is an encouragement for you to stay on the path and, in doing so, achieve what so few attain in life. Make it yours.

NOW GO LEAD

FIVE MINUTE REFLECTION

Have I stepped off the path of consistency to pursue short-term gains along the way?

Is it time for a gut check since I am going through a difficult time, with life stretching me to the limits?

WHO YOU SAY I AM

Who am I?

"You shouldn't care so much about what people think, Brandon." I think I started hearing this from my parents during elementary school; you probably heard it from someone when you were young, too. Concern for others' opinions is a common response to the human desire for acceptance. But at some point, we must gain the maturity to overlook the words and thoughts of certain people.

The explosion and sustained presence of social media clearly indicate a broad spectrum of people in the world, young and old, who are desperately enslaved to the space in their hearts they reserve for the thoughts of close friends and complete strangers alike. For myself, I have only recently discovered my own enslavement and the invisible shackles which have held me back in my own leadership journey. This revelation has set me on a path of discovery and reflection.

To understand this fully, I had to go back to the very beginning when I started my own business. I cared deeply about what people thought of me, and this commitment was a major reason for our early success. I found out if I dedicated the bulk of my time and thoughts to what potential clients were thinking about me and my business, I could very easily cater to their needs. As a result, I became known for my responsiveness and competence in my work. I was motivated by this positive feedback and thus started an endless loop in which I became increasingly motivated to listen to others' opinions and respond accordingly to meet their needs. My business grew rapidly, and I made people's opinions of me and my business the primary focus of my business strategy.

As our organization grew, I also began to care deeply about the opinions of the people within its walls. Just as with our external clients, the more I paid attention to and catered to the opinions of people in our organization, the more our employee satisfaction grew. I became known as a "great boss" and "good leader." All of these things reinforced my belief that caring about others' opinions was a key ingredient for success. But I soon found there was a hidden downside to a heavy investment in others' thoughts and opinions: they aren't always positive.

More than anything in my career, I remember the pain I would feel when a client or an employee criticized me for my shortcomings. The thought of someone out there unhappy with me turned quickly into the belief that I was a fraud. I soon noticed I was on a roller coaster of emotions, driven solely by the latest opinions of everyone in my sphere of influence. If I was having a bad day with a client, I would seek refuge in an employee who could tell me I was doing a great job. If I was having internal organizational issues, I would leave the office and find comfort in a client's words. And none of these things are bad per se, because we all need a place of refuge in life. But the truth is: I had gotten so lost in the opinions of others that I was no longer able to form a healthy view of my own identity outside of the words and opinions of the world around me.

When a leader is motivated only by the momentary, mercurial opinions of their followers, they are no longer a true leader. You must be careful not to lose your identity or your focus on the vision. Your identity as a leader is rooted in *what* you are pursuing and *why* you have chosen to lead. When you lose sight of those things, you have reached a dangerous place in the journey where darkness clouds your ability to know the true path forward. Spend some time today reminding yourself why you are leading, and get back on track toward the vision.

NOW GO LEAD

FIVE MINUTE REFLECTION

Have I tied my identity and worth as a leader solely to the opinions of others?

Have I compromised my leadership philosophy to gain the approval of those around me?

GOOD BONES

Have you ever wondered why people have walked away from your leadership?

I have observed that people find comfort under the umbrella of competent leadership. It means someone is looking out for you. It means that you can rest a little easier because you know someone else is concerned about your well-being. You only have to follow a "paper leader" one time to understand that what makes a leader desirable is much more than how you dress, what you drive, or simply being attractive. Real leaders have substance. And that **substance is found not on the surface, but in the bones.**

I recently listened to a podcast series covering the life story of Carlo Pietro Giovanni Guglielmo Tebaldo Ponzi. He was an Italian immigrant to the US in the early 1900s, and like most immigrants of the time, he crossed the ocean in pursuit of the American Dream. He struggled to make progress along his journey but was determined to find a way to make it big. Back then, there existed something called Postal Reply Coupons. They allowed a person in one country to pay for the postage of a reply to a correspondent in another country. The price of the coupon was always based on the cost of the stamp in the country it was purchased but could be redeemed for a stamp to cover the cost of postage in another country. So, in theory, it might cost less money to buy a coupon for a stamp in Europe than the actual value of a stamp in the United States, basically a form of arbitrage. Carlo came up with the idea that he could make a lot of money with the "coupon for stamp" idea and knew he had hit it big. All he needed were some investors to trust in his idea.

Carlo was able to convince a few people to get on board, and eventually the word spread. Within a few short months he had become a millionaire, and he absolutely looked the part. He dressed well, bought expensive items for his wife, and was the toast of town for time. However, he was hiding a fatal flaw to his arbitrage plan. He never really figured out a way to turn the postal coupons into cash. The US Post Office wouldn't buy the coupons, and the enormity of the coupons that would be required to pay back his investors was impractically large. By that time, he had so many people invested in his business that he couldn't possibly return all the money he had promised. Carlo had built a house of cards that could crash at any moment, but he kept up the façade for as long as possible. Eventually the storm hit, and it all came crashing down. Today the eponymous Ponzi Scheme is a long-standing reminder of the failure of Carlo's paper kingdom.

So, when we work on our leadership, we don't work so much on the surface as we do the structure. The stronger the heart, mind, and soul, the better the leader. Solomon once said that understanding is worth it, even though it costs us everything we have. Always be wary of the leader who spends more on their shoes than their books. Yes, the work on the inside takes longer and doesn't get the immediate recognition, but when the storms come (and they will), you'll be glad you put the investments in the right places

NOW GO LEAD

FIVE MINUTE REFLECTION

Take five minutes and consider your bones. Where are you putting in the work? Are you putting more effort into appearances instead of the hard work that may go unnoticed? Consider then adjust.

LOCKED IN

Are you focused on the right things?

I believe that many leaders fail to accomplish their goals at work or in life for one simple reason: a lack of focus. I see it in people who get halfway through a new diet or exercise routine. I see it when people stop short of their goals because something easier or more interesting grabs their attention. There are a thousand different reasons every day to lose focus on the task in front of you:

- A customer needs a visit.
- Someone stops by your desk for a quick chat.
- It's 11:18 and almost lunch time.
- You haven't checked Instagram in the past 30 minutes.

Each leader has their unique distractions. Accomplishing great things requires incredible discipline and sustained focus.

The funny thing about great accomplishments is no one will force you to pursue them. These goals don't fall into the "need" category. In fact, spending all your time meeting needs can easily crowd out the space required for work that rises to the level of great or meaningful.

A leader could spend their entire life simply meeting needs and never accomplish anything remarkable. To move toward a higher vision, you must occasionally set aside urgent needs to make space for important work. The real challenge of leadership isn't just keeping the organization moving — that's maintenance. The higher calling is pursuing work that moves the vision forward.

Often, the best way to focus is to force it. It may mean no phone calls, no email, or no notifications during focused time. Whatever it takes to create uninterrupted space, do it. It may sound simplistic, but if you are intent on seeing your vision become reality, you'll have to set aside the mundane to pursue what truly matters.

NOW GO LEAD

FIVE MINUTE REFLECTION

Am I carving out enough time to focus on the vision, or am I filling my days trying to keep my inbox clean?

JUST A GAME

What are you pursuing?

I'm a leader. I'm also a gamer...at least by most people's standards. I probably play video games in some form every day — and have for at least 25 years.

Recently, I started playing a puzzle game on my phone. The premise is simple: line up objects of a similar shape or color to clear them from the screen. There are dozens of games built on the same idea. As I played through the first ten to twenty levels, nothing changed much until I hit a level I could not get through.

I played it off and on for several days with no success. Finally, something dawned on me: I was pursuing the wrong goal. A splash screen at the start of the level listed a specific objective for the level. I never paid attention to it; I just kept playing the game the way I had for the first twenty levels. Once I understood the actual objective, I cleared the level immediately and moved on.

Leader, **if you believe success will come from playing the game the same way you have for several years, you're going to keep finding frustration.** The objectives are shifting, the goals are loftier, and the challenge is growing. If you want to continue experiencing organizational growth and meaningful success, you must stay aware of the rules shaping how you play the game.

We all run into barriers from time to time. You may need to lift your eyes from the weeds and see whether you're still pursuing the right objective. You likely already possess the tools and capability needed for success. You need to direct them toward the objective that truly matters.

NOW GO LEAD

<u>FIVE MINUTE REFLECTION</u>

Am I frustrated by a lack of progress?
Have I hit a wall trying to reach a new level?

LEADERSHIP SENSE

Are you in control?

Take a sheet of paper and cover your face with it. What do you see? You have put something in front of you, blocking your vision. If I asked you to hold this paper in front of your face while running down the sidewalk, you would likely harm yourself and possibly others. The absurdity of attempting such a thing is obvious.

Now think about your other senses. If you have music turned up too loud, you can't hear the whisper of truth. If emotions overrun your logic, you can't think clearly. Leaders must stay keenly aware of their senses. More frankly, **you must command your senses before you can command the masses.**

In the 1999 Sci-Fi classic, *The Matrix*, Thomas Anderson lives a mundane, workaday life as a computer programmer. At a pivotal moment, he's offered a chance to see the world in a whole new way. The world of truth. Mr. Anderson chooses the path towards enlightenment and becomes Neo, but the choice is only the beginning. Later, the sensei Morpheus attempts to teach Neo how to operate successfully within the virtual world of the Matrix. At first, Neo is too slow and always a step behind the older and wiser Morpheus. Frustrated, Neo eventually learns to command his senses and emerges as a formidable presence in the virtual world, with almost no limits on his abilities.

Leaders today resemble Mr. Anderson. We live in a world filled with distractions and diversions designed to keep us from seeing the greater truths around us. You may set aside daily moments of solitude, a good practice, but what about the actual work environment? Do you find it difficult to stay focused? We've all been guilty: one more minute on social media, one more video on YouTube, maybe just a quick text to a friend. Anything to distract us from the pressure of leadership. But the leader must have the discipline and extreme focus to guide the organization through its toughest challenges.

A leader who can't command their senses will risk missing something critical. Like Neo, we must fight for clarity and truth at every opportunity. Remove the distractions pulling you away from the leadership your team needs. Only when we command our senses can we lead with a clear focus on the vision.

NOW GO LEAD

FIVE MINUTE REFLECTION

What is the biggest distraction I am allowing into my life right now? How is it affecting my ability to lead with clarity?

A NARROW PATH

Are Your Feet Secure?

If you stay on the leadership journey long enough, you will inevitably reach places where the path begins to narrow. The incline steepens, and the margins disappear into the bottomless darkness on either side. These are the stretches where the leader must dare to walk the path many others seem to fail to navigate. On the narrowest of paths, there is room for only one person — you — with no one beside you.

I've had many moments when my own path narrowed to an uncomfortable place. I remember vividly the day one of my vice presidents walked into my office and handed over his resignation letter. Not only was he leaving our organization, but he was also going to start his own business and take as many customers and employees with him as possible.

Pain washed over me in that moment. Everything I had invested in this man, personally and financially, vanished instantly, and I was left to pick up the pieces. In many ways, it became an immediate scramble to hold onto as many customers and employees as possible. For a couple of weeks, it seemed like every other day brought another resignation and another lost client. The ground was crumbling beneath my feet, yet I knew I had to move forward.

When things hit rock bottom, it felt as if I were a thousand feet in the air, walking on a thread. I have to admit there were dark moments when giving up crossed my mind. But each morning, I would wake up and resolve to take one more step. Eventually, we made it through and rebuilt. Although I can't say I look back on that season fondly, I am proud we persevered where so many others would have packed it in. God was incredibly kind to me during those days.

Without a doubt, I know what it feels like to wonder whether your next step might be your last. I have seen other leaders in similar situations respond in different ways. Some want to widen the path. Others slow to a crawl, taking endless time to make sure each step is perfect. Some look for ways to cheat the system by looking for an alternative route to success. However, far too few leaders actually develop the discipline to teach themselves the skills to navigate the narrowest paths with enough speed and confidence to keep the organization moving forward.

I'm not saying we shouldn't make the journey easier where we can. But sometimes the leader is faced with the prospect of just grinding it out. As long as you keep finding ways to avoid the difficult situations that produce real growth, you will never develop the skills required to move your organization to the next level.

When the path narrows, your footing must be at its surest. Moving forward often depends less on your ability and more on overcoming your fears. Reflect on the successes that have brought you to this moment. You can do this, and you know what needs to be done. Just pick up your feet and start moving.

NOW GO LEAD

FIVE MINUTE REFLECTION

Am I nervous about the path before me?
Am I looking for ways to avoid the thing I know I must do?

LEADERSHIP REGRETS

What if I could go back?

Everyone has a weakness of some sort, even great leaders. Exactly what the weakness may be can vary considerably. Because great leaders often hold themselves to the highest standards, many struggle to maintain a healthy relationship with their failures or shortcomings. I have often observed regret as the monster many leaders wrestle with in their solitary moments. It's one of the biggest mental health drains a leader can face:

Why didn't I see this disaster coming?

How could I put my organization in this bad position?

Why didn't I deal with this problem sooner?

These are the questions keeping us awake at night. They can drag us down into a depression, which takes away from our ability to lead NOW. The weight of "what if" can be a miserable weight on the soul.

So, how do we get rid of regret? **The leader must live in the "now" mindset.** This is a foundational truth for a leader to learn: perspective changes everything. You are on a leadership journey. You are either just getting started, marching through the middle, or cruising into the sunset. Knowing where you are in your journey (perspective) is key to dealing with the regret monster.

At any point in the journey, you make decisions based on where you are in the moment. You only know what you know **now.** You only feel what you feel **now.** Five years ago, were you as patient, informed, wise or humble as you are today? Five weeks ago? Of course, not.

In 2018, I laid out a bold new vision for our company. One particular initiative was to start selling our professional services to the federal government. I believed our minority-owned status would give us a huge advantage in the federal marketplace. All I needed to do was find someone to head up the effort and convince my leadership team to divert the resources to float the cost while we ramped up.

I estimated we would become profitable in 18-24 months. I got buy-in from my team and hired someone with a solid work history in the space. We were rolling.

A few months into the process, we realized that landing contracts with the government takes far longer than we anticipated. On top of that, we were pursuing every opportunity we could find, so we needed to hire another person just to keep up with proposals and paperwork.

At the 18-month mark, we were barely making progress, and the costs were straining other areas of the business. Two full years in, the results were clear. I didn't have the right person leading the initiative. I had clearly underestimated the time and resources required to be successful, and we didn't have any substantial results to show for our investment. To correct course, we had to go through the painful process of layoffs. It's a scar I still feel to this day.

I wrestled with the decision for many months afterwards. Eventually I realized I wouldn't have done anything differently if I could go back. It was a risk, and it didn't work out. There was no way for me to know how it would turn out.

The point is simple: when you make necessary leadership decisions moment by moment, you can only choose based on who you are at that moment. Your "future leader" self cannot step back in time to make decisions for you. Mistakes will always be part of leadership, but they do not need to cloud your present.

Give your past self some grace. You would not have chosen differently, because you were not capable of choosing differently. You were who you were, and you are no longer the same person today (God willing). Some of the mistakes that you made are what help you to be the better and wiser leader that you are today.

NOW GO LEAD

FIVE MINUTE REFLECTION

What regrets from the past have actually shaped me into the leader I am today?

What have I learned from those decisions I made that I wish I could go back and change?

SOLITUDE OR ISOLATION?

Ever Feel like Running Away?

In one of my recent reads from 2023, *The Ruthless Elimination of Hurry*, John Mark Comer writes, "Solitude is Engagement, Isolation is Escape."

Wow. This one got me thinking. What does it even mean?

As humans and certainly as leaders, we crave time alone and away. In my executive coaching sessions, I often talk about "time to think" and "time to reflect." This kind of work happens in moments of solitude, which are difficult to carve out and even harder to make consistent.

So, there is solitude, but what exactly is isolation? Isolation is where we go when we feel the need to escape. You know this feeling: close personal relationships have drained your energy; employees won't stop bringing problems; life becomes too heavy. Suddenly, you find yourself saying, ***"I need to get out of here!"*** In isolation, we rely on our own devices, avoid accountability, and shed the "shackles" of leadership. We distract ourselves with noise — media, fantasies of escape, or anything that numbs the pressure.

Solitude, on the other hand, is where leaders go for spiritual alignment and deep introspection. Surrounded by disciplined silence, solitude becomes essential for examining the burdens of leadership away from the chaos of the battle. Here, you aren't setting aside the burden of leadership; you are digesting it, gaining perspective, and forming a plan to reengage with clarity. Solitude is steeped in personal accountability.

I began practicing moments of solitude as a teenager. It started as a spiritual discipline: reading Scripture and praying each day. I continued the practice daily. As I got married and had children, I had to wake up earlier to keep the practice alive. I eventually settled into a 5:20 a.m. wake-up, giving me plenty of time to focus, read, and meditate. My time always includes Bible reading; plus, a stack of three to four other books I read concurrently. This rhythm has played a crucial role in maintaining a healthy mental state.

However, over the years, I also began to recognize the need for some extended sabbaticals. After about ten years of running the business without a real break, I started setting aside a week away from the organization to get clarity and perspective on how things were going. In 2017, I did a two-week retreat. In 2021, I did a three-week retreat. In 2024, I took off five full weeks. Every one of these breaks was necessary, and I took full advantage of the time to heal and prepare myself for the next phase of the pursuit of the vision.

A word of warning: don't abuse the freedoms leadership offers. Organizations often encourage leaders to "spend time thinking." But it's far easier to close the office door, fire up YouTube, or catch up on some email. You might go to the lake or the beach, but if you spend the entire time distracting yourself with activities, you could end up wasting time. You must guard the time you are given.

Moments of solitude and isolation are the greatest test of leading yourself well. With no one to hold you accountable and no one to tell you what to do, how will you respond? Your ability to grow yourself and stay focused during these moments will become the defining difference between a thriving enterprise and a mediocre one. As goes the leader, so goes the organization.

NOW GO LEAD

FIVE MINUTE REFLECTION

Am I guilty of isolating under the guise of solitude?
How can I carve out a healthy amount of solitude in my
daily routine?
What habits do I need to change or develop to keep me growing
as a leader?

TRUST THE PROCESS

Is leadership really a process?

Just like any other trip you've taken, your leadership journey includes milestones. Growing leaders must understand where they are in their journey and recognize when they've moved on from novice to mastery levels of practice. While not concise and exhaustive, a typical leadership experience includes three distinct phases.

THE YOUNG LEADER

This is the stage where desire outpaces talent. You **want** to be great, you **want** to accomplish so much, but the truth is that you haven't put in the time to refine the craft.

Many young leaders stall here because they believe that zeal alone is enough to produce results. The idea that it will take time (often years) to get to the point where talent meets desire is unattractive and unappealing. You can easily spot this leader on a résumé: they will only stay at one place for one or two years. If they aren't running the company by then, they move on.

THE ARRIVING LEADER

This is the forge where authentic leaders are formed. This season requires you to be heated to the point of breaking , and you must remain moldable, humble, and endlessly resilient. The forge is where mistakes become lessons, and lessons learned become the mold you use to allow yourself to be remade.

Many leaders get stuck here because pride refuses to bend. They fail to understand that to leave the forge, every part of them must conform to the mold before they can move on. If they resist, the process of heating and breaking must start again. The sooner the arriving leader embraces humility over pride, the quicker they emerge from the forge.

THE PRACTICING LEADER

The practicing leader merges desire and talent into a powerful force for change and influence. But mature leadership requires something beyond skill: legacy. No leader rises alone. Each one stands on the shoulders of those who poured time, energy, and influence into their development. The practicing leader who refuses to prepare the next person in line commits one of the greatest leadership sins of all.

So, when you finally **DO** reach this phase, your next job is clear: return to the beginning and help a young leader enter the forge.

Navigating the phases of leadership is challenging without a guide. Find your guide or be the one for another. Commit to the process of completing the journey.

NOW GO LEAD

FIVE MINUTE REFLECTION

Where am I in my leadership journey?
What is holding me back?
How can I actively invest in the next generation of leadership?

TWENTY-FOUR

Are you first or second?

In 2003, the band Switchfoot released a song titled "Twenty-Four." It tells the story of a man determined to live life on his own terms, to the best of his ability. Yet he continually finds failure despite all his efforts. "...twenty-four failures in twenty-four tries..."

Amid all his failures, the man has an epiphany that suddenly changes his mindset about living life on his own terms. He begins to struggle, as he realizes life might be better if someone else were in charge. Yet he still finds himself offering up excuses for everything he has done. "...twenty-four reasons to admit that I'm wrong, with all my excuses still twenty-four strong..."

As his will weakens, he declares to those looking to him that by submitting to something greater than himself, he is not abdicating responsibility for his actions past, present, or future. Rather, he concedes that life might be better if he weren't calling all the shots. "...See I'm not copping out, not copping out, not copping out... Oh, I am the second man now..."

Reflecting on his decision, he understands it was only by submitting that he starts to see the world change around him. In the end, success came not from being **the** man, but from being "the second man."

The false narrative existing today is the leader must be godlike in their abilities — knowing everything, doing everything, carrying everything. But true leadership doesn't come from pretending to have all the answers. It comes from staying connected to the One who actually has them and resting in the freedom of not having to know it all.

You may discover progress begins only when you step back into second place; you will finally start to move forward.

NOW GO LEAD

FIVE MINUTE REFLECTION

Am I trying to be "The Man or The Woman?"
What does this reveal about my struggles?

TWO IMPORTANT DAYS

Do you know why you lead?

During a trip to the Ozarks, I was reminded of an old quote from Mark Twain: "The two most important days in your life are the day you are born and the day you find out why." One of these days is very easy to identify. The other often feels much more elusive. Many people spend an extraordinary portion of their lives trying to find out *"why."*

We all carry an innate desire to answer this question. It burns in our souls and pushes us to search out the answer. But there is an answer, right? Maybe it's easy to accept we must all take our own journey to uncovering "why." For a fortunate few, the answer comes early. And leadership, although undeniably difficult, is at least understood through that lens. But have you ever considered it's possible to answer the question incorrectly without even realizing it?

In that reality, you believe your leadership purpose is one thing, but *actually*, it is something altogether different. Or you long for a purpose to be something or about something not for you. Maybe you want someone else's leadership persona, their job, their relationship(s), their bank account. We drift into this trap when we search for our purpose for so long, we lose fulfillment in our own leadership path. I may not know your *"why,"* but I can tell you this: it's not a position, a job, or more money. So, where does this leave us?

The leader can never stop pursuing the *"why."* If you haven't found it yet, don't despair — your time isn't wasted. Sometimes "why" evolves, and the answer arrives at different stages of life. We must be seeking if we hope to receive the answer, and we must be willing to submit ourselves to the vision that emerges.

NOW GO LEAD

FIVE MINUTE REFLECTION

"What is my why?"
Am I pursuing my own journey, or am I instead wishing I were
leading in someone else's shoes?

DOERS AND DUDS

Do you have the courage to go alone?

I was in the middle of my first real career change when I entered the architectural engineering industry. I had spent all of my college internships and the first several years after graduation focused on a career in the auto industry. After a few years living in Detroit, I moved back to Arkansas and joined an engineering firm with several college peers who already had a three-year head start on me. I remember feeling lost, trying to understand a new environment and a new discipline. After about six months, I finally began to find my footing. I quickly learned the path to success in the architectural engineering world involved obtaining a professional engineering license, so I set out to fulfill that goal.

This process required passing a fundamentals exam before I could sit for the professional licensing exam. I teamed up with a co-worker to study for the first exam, and within seven months of starting my new career, I passed the first test. We had invested significant effort into prepping for the exam, and the success energized me. I immediately shifted my focus toward the final professional exam scheduled for that fall.

What surprised me was my co-worker's unwillingness to continue. He was worried about the effort it would take to turn the application around so quickly and the hassle of getting all the required written references from past supervisors. He also needed a break from constant studying. So I moved forward on my own, completed the process, and earned my license. It ended up being another **seven** years before my co-worker passed the exam. By then, I was already well into starting my own engineering firm.

Here is the takeaway: Some people see what they want and pursue it with everything in them. Others spend their time complaining about all the reasons they can't have it. Many times, leaders must walk the toughest stretch of the path alone. Only a courageous few choose to keep moving when others quit, when voices around them say, "You can't do this," and when a thousand challenges stand in the way. Which path will you choose?

NOW GO LEAD

FIVE MINUTE REFLECTION

Am I brave enough to pursue the right thing, even if I must go it alone?
What intentional step do I need to take today toward my goal?

SECONDS MATTER

Are you losing time?

The great philosopher Ferris Bueller once said, "Life moves pretty fast. If you don't stop and look around once in a while, you could miss it."

The passage of life is essentially a constant progression of choices. Each choice is an exercise of trading your most valuable asset for something you deem worthy. You might ask, "What is my most valuable asset?" *Hint: It's not your money.*

Your most valuable asset is your time. It is yours alone. Yours to share. Yours to spend. The only control you have is how to use it. If you choose not to do anything with it, time moves on without you.

Since time is irreplaceable, we must make wise choices with what we do. Few things are more tragic than wasted time. You can never recover it, and yet we often assume it is unlimited. Shockingly, we learn it is not.

A short-sighted person has a limited view of time's worth. However, a person with vision understands not only the moment, but also what the long-term cost of a given choice may be over the course of a lifetime. Many consider happiness in life as the ability to accept the choices we have made. On the other hand, people who are disillusioned with life are often riddled with regret over choices they wish they could undo. So you can see that making good choices is kind of a big deal!!

I hope you're beginning to grasp the gravity of the choices we make each day. You can't appreciate the weight of your decisions until you gain the perspective to see life as it truly is — **an opportunity**. It's an opportunity to use the time you have to make the world a better place and enrich the lives of the people who have been put in your path. If you have anything meaningful to offer the people in your sphere of influence, it's your time. Give it generously and intentionally, and you will start to see your leadership grow.

NOW GO LEAD

FIVE MINUTE REFLECTION

Are my choices as a leader giving me the best return on my investment? Am I investing in intentional activities that are growing my leadership and my team's lives?

DARE TO LEAD

Will you answer the bell?

Welcome to leadership. The spotlight is on **you** now. Every success becomes an expectation, but a single failure feels unforgivable. When the leader falls, everyone watches with bated breath. They see the leader broken and on the ground. A crowd forms; some hurl insults, others look on in fear, and many gloat. But they all want to know one thing: How is this going to turn out?

I've only been punched in the face once in my life. Eighth-grade football was a bit of a Lord of the Flies arrangement. Practice started in the fourth period, right after lunch, so we were expected to eat quickly, get to the locker room, and be dressed for practice before drills started. The coaches never showed up during this prep time, so we were basically a bunch of teenage boys running amok in the field house for about 30 minutes with no one to oversee our activities.

We were, however, expected to be "ready to go" once the coach showed up. To start, we were supposed to line up for warm-ups and calisthenics. Due to the limited space in the field house, that meant four boys across and eight deep. No one wanted to be in the back of the room (it smelled terrible), so there was always a little jockeying for position to be close to the front. Unwritten rules governed this chaos, one of them being: **if you were first in line, you had rights.**

One day, I reached the line at the exact same time as another kid named Ronnie. We both started arguing, each convinced we were right. Meanwhile, the rest of the team had already lined up, which meant whoever backed down would have to head to the dreaded back of the room. I shoved Ronnie aside, told him to get lost, and began doing my stretches. I never saw the punch coming.

A warm sensation spread across my face, and the dawn of apprehension swept over me as I realized this had escalated beyond what I was prepared to deal with. Ronnie was much bigger than me, a good forty pounds heavier, and I knew I wouldn't win. The entire room had stopped stretching. All eyes were on us. I could feel the heat of the moment closing in.

So, I did the only reasonable thing I could think of: I walked to the back of the room.

I lived to fight another day.

If I remember correctly, Ronnie eventually got his butt kicked by a couple of guys who were looking out for me. I still wonder whether I made the right decision to walk away, but I'll never forget how it made me feel in that moment.

The leader's uncanny ability to pick themselves up off the mat and face their opponent for another round is something baffling to the watchers. Why would anyone willingly step back into the ring after being knocked down? When the leader fails, there is fallout. People question your ability to lead. Doubt seeps in.

In those moments of failure, an internal war erupts in the leader's tormented heart. On one side stands the person you are right now. On the other stands the leader you believe you can become. *Everyone* sees your present failure; only *you* can see the future where the vision becomes reality. But to reach this place, you must choose to move. There will be a story to tell one day. Forgiveness will come. Redemption will come. But only if you keep getting up. Are you down for the count?

I've fallen more times than I can remember. If you lead long enough, you will fall too. However, your leadership story only ends when you decide you won't take the next hard step.. Today, I **dare** you to get back up and keep fighting.

NOW GO LEAD

FIVE MINUTE REFLECTION

Do I have what it takes to pick myself up and try again?

DESPERATION

Have you ever been desperate?

It's astonishing what people will do in desperate situations. I would guess many of your greatest achievements, or worst regrets, came during a moment of desperation. Truthfully, we are all susceptible to doing the unthinkable when the right pressure hits at the wrong time.

Because clear thinking is such a critical skill for leaders, it is of utmost importance for them to recognize when desperation is clouding their judgment.

Desperation is a fascinating emotion because in many ways, it exists entirely in our minds. This means your sense of desperation in any given situation may not be relevant to me. You might be desperate to get the right anniversary gift for your spouse two hours before dinner, but I'm not concerned at all because my anniversary is six months away.

Certainly, desperation has a personal element. In addition to specific circumstances driving us to desperation, it's also the degree of control we believe we have in any given situation. Sometimes we feel desperate yet still understand we can change our circumstances. In other situations, desperation rises to another level when we feel trapped against impending doom or seemingly unchangeable circumstances.

The moments of greatest desperation in my own journey usually involved money, or perhaps more appropriately, the lack of it. This seemed to be a recurring theme in the early years of the business, as customers paid slowly and we regularly hit the limits of our line of credit with the bank. I went home without a paycheck a couple of times, and I remember those moments well. In those seasons of desperation, we took any work we could find, even if it meant working for some dubious characters or taking on some risky projects. We ultimately climbed out of the hole, but the consequences stayed with us. We usually regretted agreeing to some of the work we took on, and no one was happy working for the clients who treated us poorly. In hindsight, I can't say I would do anything differently, but I now understand far more clearly how desperation can push us into decisions we would never consider in calmer moments.

The leader is tasked with handling all the most difficult and heavy burdens of the entire organization. It's part of the job, and to some degree, the leader can get used to having their feet in the fire. Even so, there will be persistent weekly and monthly "issues" because solutions remain elusive. Pressure mounts. People want the leader to be the hero and do the impossible.

These are the moments that push and stretch the leader the most; they challenge us to grow and learn. But this is also where the leader must take the greatest care: ***Decision-making is often at its weakest when desperation is at its peak.***

During seasons of desperation, I have learned several lessons that continue to protect me from poor decisions that I would later regret

1. Stay hyper aware of your state of desperation. You are making daily decisions with long-term consequences that may cascade through your organization for years.
2. Understand why you feel desperate. Sometimes desperation is this fuzzy, unclear thing in the back of your head, pulling the strings without you realizing what is going on.
3. Work to resolve the source of your desperate situation. Seek help from a trusted advisor or your closest peers. You may need to retreat, step away, or otherwise change your environment to gain clarity.
4. Delay important decisions until you feel free from the pressure of desperation. Even a small buffer of time can restore clear thinking.

NOW GO LEAD

FIVE MINUTE REFLECTION

How do I handle desperate situations?
Do I have a plan to guide me through tough moments, or am
I making it up as I go?

THE WELL SOUL

Is your soul well?

I was fifteen years old when I first heard the story of Horatio Spafford. I was sitting in the Thorncrown Chapel in Eureka Springs, Arkansas, on a spring day, and I remember being surrounded by the stunning beauty of the Ozarks.

Horatio was a successful lawyer who invested heavily in Chicago real estate in the late 1860s. The Great Fire of 1871 destroyed most of his property, financially ruined him, and left him further impoverished during the Panic of 1873. Around this time, he planned a family trip to participate in an evangelistic campaign in Europe. At the last moment, Horatio had to send his wife and daughters ahead of him while he tended to some urgent business.

During the voyage, the ship collided with another sea vessel and sank almost instantly. Horatio's four daughters drowned, and his wife was rescued and taken on to Europe. As he traveled to meet his wife, the captain of the ship notified him when their ship crossed the waters where his children had died. It was there in that moment of grief Horatio penned the words to the now famous hymn, "It is Well with my Soul."

Even now, the story moves me as deeply as it did when I first heard it. It remains a profound reminder of the importance of soul health for the leader.

Inevitably, the leader endures seasons where waves of loss, failure, and circumstance crash relentlessly against their soul. In those moments, you will feel every emotion accompanying uncertainty. But the question remains: *is it well with your soul?*

A leader's soul is not made well because of accomplishments or favorable circumstances. It is well **despite** them. Within a well soul is a steady, unwavering stillness, allowing the leader to put even the darkest days into context and move forward with unflinching resolve. Your soul becomes well when you release what you cannot control and accept your limitations. It is the peace that comes from accepting what is and continuing to believe that there are better days ahead.

NOW GO LEAD

<u>FIVE MINUTE REFLECTION</u>

What is the state of my soul?
Do I have the most important matters settled in my life?
How can I be sure to lead with a steady soul regardless of what comes my way?

BETTER OR BITTER

How do you want to proceed?

In the aftermath of extraordinary difficulty, I have heard it said: You can become better, or you can become bitter. For me, this statement captures the true essence of resilient leadership. If you can't get this one right, you'll never rise to the higher levels of the leadership journey. Tim McGraw once sang, *"bitterness keeps you from flyin."* He's not wrong.

I remember when our company landed its first big project. It was the largest fee to date and represented the culmination of a lot of effort earning the opportunity. We worked extremely hard on the project, but despite our best efforts, the building had some lingering problems requiring ongoing attention after construction.

We spent many months on site working to resolve problems, and we were close to finishing when the client called to say they were done. They didn't want us on the project anymore. What followed was a long, draining conflict that cost us financially — and cost us the relationship with an excellent customer.

I was devastated. I felt we had been treated unfairly and abandoned. My response? Bitterness. I wanted nothing good for the people who had walked away from us.

But my bitterness didn't stay contained. It quickly grew into cynicism. I started assuming the worst about others. I trusted less. I led with suspicion instead of hope. Eventually, I realized this bitterness was holding me back, poisoning my leadership, and shrinking my capacity.

So I made a choice.

I took ownership of what I could.

I learned from the experience.

And *I became better.*

The **bitter** leader remembers all the reasons for the failure. They keep a list of those who wronged and hurt them. They believe their success has been stymied and stolen by others. They insist that their lack of progress is the world's fault, not their own.

The **better** leader remembers the same failures — but responds differently. They forgive. They release anger. They believe that success is still possible as long as they grow. They will soar because they have grown strong enough to see the word from the right perspective.

Bitterness often begins in innocent ways. Maybe you were wronged or hurt and you long for justice. That desire for justice screams in your head, demanding others be held accountable for their actions. Eventually, however, you must recognize the difference between what you can control and what you cannot. Owning your part and releasing your demand for justice is the first step in becoming better. Make the choice today to become a better leader by leaving your bitterness behind.

NOW GO LEAD

FIVE MINUTE REFLECTION

Where have I let bitterness take root?
Is it focused on a person?
Is it focused on a situation?
Is it focused on God?
What is it that could be holding me back from soaring to the higher
levels of leadership?

MAKE IT HAPPEN

Are you trying to make it happen?

I'm a doer — most leaders are. In our culture, we look to leaders to get things done. Leaders who don't produce often get pushed to the sidelines because "we need results." Longer resumes are much more impressive than short ones.

Actually, I am starting to believe that our obsession with outcomes pushes us to force results when waiting serves us better. Ideas like "something is better than nothing" or "if I don't do something, no one else will" may sound noble, but they can be dangerous. If we truly understood how often we make mistakes, we might realize we'd be better off not doing something more frequently. **The leader doesn't always have to be the one to make it happen.**

Reflect on this: How many times has "making it happen" put you in a worse situation instead of improving your circumstances? You have a moment of crisis in your life, a relationship breaks, your faith feels tested. Does your urge to "make it happen" increase in times of crisis or organizational chaos? You find yourself saying, "I need to do something, or this won't end well!"

Several years ago, we decided to add on to our house. If you've ever gone through a renovation, you know it's a chaotic process. For several weeks during construction, the back wall of my house was nothing more than a clear sheet of plastic. Dust everywhere. Constant noise. Dinner on a card table. Pure madness.

Because of my engineering background, I decided to do the electrical wiring myself. For the most part, it went fine, and I learned a lot through the process. However, towards the end of the project, emotions ran high, and we were all ready to just be done. The final electrical inspection was being held up because I needed to install some outdoor lights. The siding contractor had not cut any holes in the aluminum soffit, so I was faced with either figuring it out myself or waiting a few days for someone else to do it.

After staring at the blank soffit for a few minutes one afternoon, I convinced myself that I could do the job. I went to Home Depot, spent a few hundred dollars on parts and tools, and jumped right in.

Thirty seconds later, I completely mangled the aluminum soffit and ruined some ancillary siding as well. We had to order more soffit materials, which delayed the project for another week. It was a mess.

It may feel counterculture, but *nothing* might be exactly what you need right now. What your followers may interpret as passivity can actually be a profound demonstration of maturity — the wisdom to know when restraint is better than force. Here are some questions to ask in these moments:

- Do I truly need to act right now, or am I feeling panic?
- Can I be ok with waiting to gain greater clarity about how to move forward?
- By acting, am I possibly preventing someone else from having an opportunity to elevate?

I dare you to take a few minutes this week to be still. No phone. No email. Just breathing, listening, and letting your soul settle. Remind your heart and your soul you can lead with authority often by choosing not to act at all.

NOW GO LEAD

FIVE MINUTE REFLECTION

Consider the entirety of your life — your job, your most important relationships, your journey through life, and even your past three months.

Are you where you are because you've been patient and wise, or is your life more a result of you striving to "make it happen?"

ACRID AGREEMENTS

I agreed to do what?

When I speak to anyone about leadership, I always start with a discussion on leadership philosophy. It's essential preparation before the journey begins, because your philosophy sets expectations, direction, and tone for the path ahead. However, I have learned something important: it's one thing to *have* a leadership philosophy or a philosophy about life. It is another thing entirely to *live* the beliefs you claim to hold.

Being the natural teachers that some leaders are, we will have a steady stream of people in our lives asking for clarity and direction. Consequently, as a "wise and mature" leader, we always offer sage advice to help move everyone in the right direction. What I have found is that often we believe our ideas about life and leadership are good for others, but we have a hard time applying them to ourselves. We say, "You should do this," or "It's clear what should happen here," yet we have no intention of dealing with our own life issues in the same way. It seems entirely too difficult, right?

There is the story in the Bible where King David commits adultery, then arranges the murder of the woman's husband. At first, he seems to get by relatively unscathed. Many months pass, and eventually one of the prophets comes to him with a story:

"There were two men in the same city—one rich, the other poor. The rich man had huge flocks of sheep and herds of cattle. The poor man had nothing but one little female lamb, which he had bought and raised. It grew up with him and his children as a member of the family. It ate off his plate and drank from his cup and slept on his bed. It was like a daughter to him. One day, a traveler *dropped in on the rich man. He was too stingy to take an animal from his own herds or flocks to make a meal for his visitor, so he took the poor man's lamb and prepared a meal to set before his guest. Da-vid exploded in anger. "As surely as God lives," he said to the prophet, "the man who did this must die! He must repay the lamb four times over for his crime and his stinginess!" The prophet then said to David, "You yourself are the man!"*[1]

Ouch, I bet that hit hard! You can almost feel the weight of the moment. Here's the point: There are very likely some obvious, glaring issues you are facing right now that you are continuing to ignore. **What you have actually done is made some acrid agreements with yourself.** We often decide (sometimes subconsciously,) that what is good and right for others does not apply to ourselves, and we learn to cope and hide our own issues while still counseling others on how they should "break free" and "change their situation."

Common internal agreements often sound like: "It'll always be this way," "I can't change it," "Success is for everyone else, not me," or "This is just my lot in life." Hear me on this: *These things are holding you back*, and they will keep coming up over and over until you finally de-cide to confront and dismantle them. They function as self-made prisons — for your soul, your leadership, and your future.

A major step forward for any leader is learning to align the hardest parts of life with the reality of their beliefs. This is the beginning of au-thenticity. This is the refining work of leadership.

NOW GO LEAD

---

1   2 Samuel 12:1-7

FIVE MINUTE REFLECTION

What bitter agreements have I made with myself?
What deep-rooted agreements are holding me back?
How can I change these and break free from them?

A PREPARED HEART

Am I prepared for this?

You must prepare your heart to lead. I've let a lot of things sneak up on me over time. Sometimes it's been a meeting; other times, an important holiday or anniversary. I think we've all experienced the dread and anxiety involved in approaching an event and trying to wing it or bluff our way through, hoping we can survive without too much collateral damage to our reputation and image.

In the 2004 comedy classic *Anchorman: The Legend of Ron Burgundy*, Ron is on a first date with his co-worker. He is approached by the bar's owner, who interrupts their meal and implores Ron to play the jazz flute. Ron initially objects and demurs, stating that he wasn't prepared. However, with a little coaxing from the patrons, he runs up on stage and pulls a flute from up his sleeve (it was there the whole time) and completely impresses the audience. It's done for humorous effect, but if you take a moment and consider, it is abundantly clear that Ron has put in many hours of practice to get to this point in his life. **He was prepared for the moment.**

Today, I am reminding you that leadership is a daily activity. Many days, your innate skills and talents can carry you through the mundane and trivial; however, you can rarely predict when the challenging days will come upon you. If you aren't preparing your heart, mind, body, and soul for leadership, you risk getting blindsided by an incoming haymaker that could put you down for the count.

So, how should you prepare your heart to lead?

First, start the morning with some form of meditation. Before you pick up the phone. Before you read your email. Just take those first twenty minutes with a cup of coffee and get your mind straight, even if it means being a few minutes late to the office.

Keep a handy list of the people in your organization and think about them. What does each individual need from you today? If you come across a name that gives you pause or tugs at your heart, take a minute and understand why. Am I avoiding an important conversation? Is there a conflict I need to resolve? Have I been meeting my own expectations for leadership about this person? Am I leading them well? Commit in the moment to lead each of your people well in the day ahead.

Next, step back and visualize your organization. Are the critical functions operating well? Is there a team, a group, a process that gives you pause? What is it you need to address today to protect the future of your organization?

Lastly, remind yourself of the vision. Tell yourself why you are leading and visualize the outcomes the organization needs to achieve in the coming day. It is only with a well-prepared heart that you will be able to face unexpected challenges and shepherd the organization safely to the fulfillment of the vision.

NOW GO LEAD

FIVE MINUTE REFLECTION

What am I doing every day to prepare my heart for leadership?
Am I putting in the work that guarantees I will have a chance to be
successful when the moment arrives?

THE MAKEOVER

What are you building?

I am a sucker for home makeover shows. It doesn't really matter who the host is or where the location is; the concept is generally the same. It's an effort to take something old and rundown and turn it into something new and beautiful. Even with such a simple concept, there is a formula for these shows that makes them work. Inevitably, an unexpected twist will be uncovered during the process. It could be an unforeseen structural problem, a budget issue, or maybe undiscovered infestations. One way or another, the owner of the makeover must overcome the biggest challenge to see the dream realized.

Let's talk about your leadership for a minute. You decide to put in the work to become the leader you want to be. You have some vague ideas of what needs the most attention, and you begin the journey. Generally, you are okay with this process because it aligns with your expectations. But suddenly you realize you'll have to knock down some structural walls to complete the process. You're going to have to visit some dark places and confront some serious issues you weren't really ready to address. "This isn't in the budget!" You hoped you'd be able to get by without having to deal with it. You know it's going to be painful, and you are left with the big decision: "Am I willing to see this through, or will I just walk away?"

Here is the truth: At the outset of our journey, our initial ideas about the final shape of our leadership are very likely wrong, or at least too small. You thought it was going to be easy and you could find a nice little cozy place for yourself. The reality is your leadership journey is going to take a much larger toll on you than you perhaps were ready for, but it also means there are much greater rewards waiting for you on the other side. You become, not the leader you thought you needed to be, but the leader you should be.

Let me urge you to have the courage to finish the work you have started. Don't delay; the costs only increase over time, and don't walk away when the end is within your sights.

NOW GO LEAD

<u>FIVE MINUTE REFLECTION</u>

What do I need to do to move forward with my leadership skills?
Am I trying to find a way to finish the project without doing the work that needs to be done?
If so, what steps can I take to overcome the hurdle that is before me?

DIFFERENT IS THE NEW OATMEAL

What's in your oatmeal?

Oatmeal is perhaps one of the blandest dishes humans have ever concocted. It is, at its essence, oats that have been bloated with water and then heated to make them more palatable. The very best and very worst bowls of oatmeal all look the same. There is nothing either distinct or remarkable about a bowl of oatmeal, but it will get the job done when you're hungry.

There is enormous pressure on leaders today. We are asked to be at once a visionary, a shepherd, a counselor, and a manager. We are expected to be firm, gentle, bombastic, humble, shrewd, and forgiving. And if that wasn't enough, we must find ways to stand out among the myriad of would-be leaders. We must create a brand, write a book, give a TED Talk, and have at least a million followers on social media. Is your brand of leadership getting noticed? That's the new definition of modern leadership. Or put another way, **being different is the new oatmeal.**

Not too long ago, following the great wars of the early 20th century, the command-and-control leadership style was the norm. As the decades passed, we began to focus more on human relations and transformational leadership. At the turn of the century, we were focused on servant leadership and emotional intelligence. Today, we are asked to be data-driven leaders who are highly adaptable. In the near future, we will be outsourcing our leadership decision-making to artificial intelligence; in fact, it's already happening.

Each of these trends in leadership was often kick-started by some author with a "revolutionary" or "radical" idea. Every hip leader in the country would get on board, and eventually the zeitgeist would adapt. And then, just about the time everyone had figured out and spent the money to implement, the idea became outdated. Today, there seems to be so many new ideas coming at us every day that you can't really tell the difference between what's truly meaningful and beneficial or simply different.

As a leader and organizationally, do you find yourself conforming to the latest leadership fad so seem relevant or popular? Are you afraid to take a stand or be different because it'll turn the spotlight on you? It seems that being different is now the new way to conform. Traditional and timeless seem to be out of sync with modern culture. Instead, we are asked to be relevant leaders within organizations that constantly affirm the latest definitions of normal. I am not suggesting that we don't strive to stay current, but we need to be aware when we begin to erode our principles in favor of trying to be attractive. In doing so, we become neither distinct nor remarkable, like the gray, forgettable bowl of the mushy tuff.

I believe in many ways, the elite leaders are the ones who stick to the timeless and pursue the eternal. Don't sacrifice what makes your leadership distinct in pursuit of a sphere of influence that only disappears when you can no longer keep up. Instead of just getting the job done, like a bowl of oatmeal, give them something that will change their life.

NOW GO LEAD

FIVE MINUTE REFLECTION

Is my leadership timeless or just timely?
Am I leading for approval or leading from the heart?

FIGHT THE JADED SPIRIT

What does it mean to be jaded?

Jaded is what happens when the harsh realities of leadership collide with the ideals of your vision. The jaded leader has lost their enthusiasm for the future because they begin to question whether what they are doing really matters. I've been there, and trust me, it's a tough place to live.

At some point, your jaded soul leads you to a crisis of belief. It's a profoundly existential moment when everything you once held true is forced to stand against the ugly reality of a broken world. But I have learned, however, that leaders with the most longevity know the secret sauce for winning this battle every time. Since I know your leadership will inevitably come across this as well, it makes sense that we take a minute to discuss, practically, how to handle this part of the journey. If you can't get up every morning and fight against this monster, it'll eventually cause you to walk away from the very things you once loved.

In the movie *Everything Everywhere All at Once*, Evelyn is a small business owner whose life seems to be failing in every possible way; her marriage is crumbling, her business is being targeted by the IRS, and her relationship with her daughter, Joy, is strained. Through a strange series of events, Joy and Evelyn both experience many parallel versions of their lives, leading them to wonder whether anything they do is actually worth the effort.

In a moment of crisis, Joy says, "It feels good, doesn't it? If nothing matters, then all the pain and guilt you feel for making nothing of your life goes away." It's a seductive lie: if we decide nothing matters, you never have to feel the sting of failure or the weight of unmet expectations. It's a very nihilistic point of view, but unfortunately, one that is all too common among struggling leaders.

So how do we win this battle?

I find it best to fight this monster in the mornings before I start the day and, in the evenings, before I go to bed. At the start of each day, remind yourself of your successes and say them out loud. It's a little weird, but trust me, it works. Next, you must remind yourself of why you are leading because if the reason is solid, it's worth getting up every day and taking up the charge to move forward. Lastly, don't run and hide from the jaded monster at night by jumping into a streaming binge or doom-scrolling on social media. The beast will wait until you are finished and then go in for the kill once you're too tired to fight back. You must keep vigilant. If you keep showing up day by day, the spirit will eventually leave you alone...for a while.

IT'S TIME TO FIGHT BACK! Let your love for what first got you on this journey lead you to the truth: **What you are doing matters!** Your team is following you because they believe in you. Everyone fails occasionally, but it doesn't mean the next win isn't right around the corner. Time to kick some jaded butt.

NOW GO LEAD

FIVE MINUTE REFLECTION

Where have I let the jaded monster turn my truth into lies?
Am I losing my ability to love and lead because the jaded monster
has told me it just doesn't matter?
What specific examples can I think of where I am making an impact
in the lives of those around me?

THE MOMENT

When was your moment?

I speak so much about clarity and perspective that I sometimes forget what things were like before I began to have a clear vision for my life. Every leader needs this. A leader without a defining moment of clarity in their life is like a spinning compass. They have no true direction and move forward based on the wind's direction at the moment. Their organizations wander and sputter but never seem to make any real progress. It's a sad existence for far too many.

But you ask, what is "the moment?"

The moment may look a little different for everyone, but at its core, it is the inflection point in your life when everything you thought you knew about existence and the universe becomes insignificant, and you see life for the first time for what it really is. For some, the moment comes through pain: a failure, a betrayal, a diagnosis, a loss you didn't see coming. For others, it comes through success that still feels empty - the promotion, the milestone, the applause that doesn't satisfy. Sometimes it arrives in a quiet instant: a conversation, a sentence in a book, a prayer you can't un-pray. However it comes, the pattern is the same: the old story collapses, and a truer one takes its place. The circumstances may not change overnight, but you do. You stop living reactively and start living deliberately. You don't get a perfect map, but you do get true north - and from that point forward, you lead with direction instead of drift.

If you've ever met someone and experienced "love at first sight," you might get a sense of what I'm talking about. You walk into a room and behold a picture of beauty that captivates your soul. Your worries and anxiety seem to melt away, and your entire existence and reason for living coalesce on the face of a complete stranger. Someone you have never met but would give all you own to share the next moments of your life with them.

In his book *Greenlights*, Matthew McConaughey describes the moment he met his future wife, Camila. He was mixing drinks at a party and saw her across the room. He had recently given up on trying to find "the one" and was therefore caught totally by surprise when Camila came into his vision for the first time. Later, he was in conversation with her when one of his friends came to tell him it was time to go home. Without ever breaking her gaze, he held his hand up towards his friend and told him to wait. Camila had so enraptured his soul he couldn't bother to look away for even a second to acknowledge his friend. He was all in, and there was nothing anyone could do from that moment forward to draw him away. He had finally found the one.

We are talking about powerful stuff. I am talking about the moment in your life when you understand why you are called to lead. When you knew without any doubt you finally grabbed hold of something worth having, and you couldn't wait to share it with the rest of the world. It is your reason for leading and your reason for living. It will carry you through hard times and motivate you to continue when others would walk away.

Share your moment with someone today. Tell the story of why you lead and memorialize the moment when you finally saw the path for the vision.

NOW GO LEAD

FIVE MINUTE REFLECTION

When was my moment?
Am I trying to lead based on my own vague notions of leadership
from a book, or do I know in my soul why I lead?
What is my reason for leading?

THE BURDEN

What's on your back?

In the movie, *The Legend of Bagger Vance*, the main character told Junuh: "Ain't a soul on this entire earth ain't got a burden to carry that he doesn't understand." I love this line because it reminds me leaders are just like any other person. We all have burdens unique to us that we just don't understand. For most of us, it is the thing we see as the barrier to greater leadership. It is the thing we wish we could change most about our circumstances or our past. It is the burden that seems to stick with us, no matter where we go and how much we try to run away from it. This burden can sometimes become a source of envy for the leader. We see another leader who appears unburdened by panic attacks before public speaking, or the leader who seems to have a perfect home life, and we believe that if we didn't have these problems, there would be nothing holding us back.

But it is the burden, and the constant presence of the burden, reminding us why we lead. Someone who has no familiarity with pain and difficulty cannot effectively lead those who are suffering. The truth is the burden is not holding you back but actually giving you the ability to lead well.

My encouragement for you today is to leverage your burden into your leadership. Who needs to know what you've been carrying, and how can you help those following you to navigate through the dark places your burden has taken you? I hope that you can start to gain perspective on this in your journey. Your burden is yours, but your leadership is for the world.

NOW GO LEAD

<u>FIVE MINUTE REFLECTION</u>

What is my burden? You won't have to think about this for too long;
you know exactly what it is.

Write down the burden on a piece of paper and reflect on it
for a moment.

How has this burden played a role in shaping my leadership?
Many times, as leaders, we seek answers to our problems, but we
may never know why we were asked to carry our *specific burden.*

MOLDABLE

Are you soft?

We often think about the leader's responsibility to grow and shape individuals in the organization, but the leader must also be in a constant state of personal growth. Who or what shapes the leader? The leader is shaped by circumstances, people, and the hard lessons encountered along the journey. Over the years of my own journey, it has become clear to me that **a soft heart is the key to longevity in leadership.**

Think for a minute about the multitude of man-made creations in existence: beautiful pieces of artwork, breathtaking concrete structures, steel bridges, and the simplest pieces of jewelry. All were once subject to a creator, and all had to be in a moldable state while the work was being done. In this moldable state, they do not nearly represent what they will one day become. They are not strong; they are weak. They are not yet beautiful, but in process. They are not finished; they are emerging. If any of these creations are set too quickly or are not subjected to the process of purification, they must be broken down and remade.

Let me encourage you to keep your heart soft as you move forward. Let's take a look at some practical steps to keep your heart ready to lead and learn:

1. Stay vulnerable with those closest to you.
2. Fight hard against pride, no matter how much you learn and achieve.
3. Ask for and accept feedback regularly from those you are leading..
4. Stay emotionally relevant and open to love.

Our culture seems to embrace the hard and leathery leader, but the powerful, beautiful, and breathtaking leader you will become is an inevitable outcome when you choose to keep your mind open and your heart soft.

NOW GO LEAD

FIVE MINUTE REFLECTION

In my rush to arrive, have I passed up some important lessons which are breaking me instead of molding me?

ABOUT FAITH

Can we talk about faith?

There are many times as a leader when you have nothing to go on but pure faith. You may call it other things: gut, instinct, or a feeling. But at some level, you are relying on something obviously etheric but definitely real. Faith may be hard to define, but I love this definition: *[it] is being sure of what we hope for and certain of what we do not see.* This sums up what faith is to me. You have something you hope for: a world where you've achieved your vision. And you believe in it even though it doesn't yet exist.

I think about everything I've experienced in my life and as a leader, and I can't help but feel like something is broken about the human condition. There have been moments over the last several years that have taken me to my knees. I'm talking about getting hit so hard that I found myself weeping when no one was looking -literally bent over, holding my knees and begging God to keep me from having to face the next day. Unfortunately, you're going to have those moments along your journey, too. I wish it wasn't true, but I'm telling you this so you can be prepared. The question is, where are you going to turn in these moments?

I ask because, in my experience, when things get rough, a lot of your support tends to disappear. In these moments, you're going to have nothing but yourself and your faith. This is a very real moment for a leader. When it comes down to those critical make-or-break moments, are you going to survive? Sometimes you realize you've put your faith in the wrong things or people. You might be able to bounce back from a couple of hits, but the more disappointments you have, the more you might find yourself questioning whether faith is even worth it.

You might not ever hear many people talk about this, but strong faith is essential to successful leadership. You must start by knowing your faith, and then, just like any other discipline, you must strengthen it. Faith is not strengthened by material gain and increasing levels of influence. Faith grows when you test what you believe about life against the harshest realities you will face along the journey. It is a hard road to grow your faith, but when tested faith meets powerful leadership, you will be able to overcome almost anything...

NOW GO LEAD

<u>FIVE MINUTE REFLECTION</u>

What does faith mean to me?
What do I believe in that I can't always see with my eyes?
What hope sustains me when all else fails?

SELF-MADE LEADERS

Did you get here on your own?

Not trying to brag too much, but I consider myself to be a pretty smart and competent individual. I can drive a car, wire up a house, and operate a forklift. Having said that, I am reminded of the many times in my life when I have encountered something new and unknown. Something that, in retrospect, is almost laughably trivial but, in the moment, seems daunting and honestly scary.

I remember the first time I ever had edamame. I was with a client, and a dish was presented to our table. I thought it was a bowl of pea pods. I dove right in and popped an entire pod in my mouth. I immediately realized these were, in fact, not pea pods, and I was going to have to spit out the half-masticated pod. I was embarrassed as I watched the guy across from me remove the edamame from the pod **before** eating it.

We've all been there before. There's something everyone seems to be good at, but you aren't. You envy those people who have a key part of life figured out that you know nothing about. If you have ever tried to do some drywall finishing or maybe make a dessert that looked amazing on Pinterest, you know exactly what I'm talking about. What started out with enthusiasm and optimism ended in tears, frustration, and a few words that made the paint on the walls turn a little red. That's not to mention the mess you must clean up, too.

Today, let me remind you of something: **you aren't meant to figure out leadership on your own**. If you want your leadership journey to be successful, you must acknowledge that to continue growing as a leader, you need someone to come alongside you and show you the way. Instead, leave behind the false idea of an independent, self-made leader, and embrace leadership learned in community. Otherwise, you're headed for a big mess you might not be able to clean up.

There is strength to be found in humility. I encourage you today to seek out the help you need most as a leader. Invite others into your life who are willing to illuminate your path rather than fumble along in the dark by yourself. You will soon find the best way to strengthen your leadership is to weaken your reliance on yourself.

NOW GO LEAD

FIVE MINUTE REFLECTION

How could my leadership grow if I find another who can walk this path with me?

Who can I reach out to that would encourage me and make me a better leader?

THE THIEF

Where is your joy?

Theodore Roosevelt once said "Comparison is the thief of joy". I'm sure it held relevance in his day, but it feels so much more profound over a hundred years later. A leader must have a heart that is ready to lead. Yet, there are so many external attacks coming at us daily and so many emotions threatening to undermine our entire journey; it is often hard to narrow down exactly what is clouding our hearts on any given day. I believe comparison is a sinister root of constant struggle for a leader, and it seems we have no end of information these days against which to compare ourselves: compensation, possessions, influence, competitor businesses. Not only that, but it also seems that our successes are measured only by our ability to surpass others on their own path. Sadly, along the path of constant comparisons, we find our joy and ability to lead are regularly hindered by where we rank relative to others.

Isn't it strange that I can enjoy my job and find daily fulfillment, only to be completely derailed when I find out someone else is making a few more bucks than I am for the same job? Similarly, I can feel passionate, joyful, and engaged in my leadership, but when I discover someone else is experiencing greater organizational growth and more LinkedIn clicks, my whole world starts to darken.

Think about this for a moment. If there was no one else out there to compare yourself against, what would success and joy look like to you? If your current salary is meeting your needs and many of your wants, why is it that your joy seems to be tied to getting more and more? This is an important issue for the leader to settle in their life. Not the issue of the desire for improvement. In fact, I believe desire is a fundamental emotion driving us to succeed. No, the issue I am talking about is having our hearts tied to an ever-changing, ever-increasing scale of "enough." Enough money, enough influence, enough better than my peers, enough to impress my family, enough to fill the gaping hole in my heart that seems to get bigger the more I throw at it.

Hear me on this, leader: If you let comparisons define your reality, your leadership, and your sphere of influence, you are placing them at extreme risk. When you become too focused on your own achievement, you will start steering your organization down dangerous, potentially catastrophic paths in pursuit of your own fulfillment. This is not the path of the true leader. You must understand there is no end to the comparison game, and true gains in the journey come when you begin to lay down your life for the people you are leading. It is in humility that the leader becomes the strongest and finds lasting joy. Today, commit to ignoring the impulse to compare, and instead let your desires for achievement be the fuel to take you on the journey that is unique to you.

NOW GO LEAD

FIVE MINUTE REFLECTION

Have I let constant comparison creep into my ability to lead well? What comparisons are leading me to doubt my ability to lead or lower my concepts of self-worth?

NOT AN OPTION

What's holding you back?

There's a lot to unpack there. Let's look at it another way. Picture, if you will, a bookshelf in the grand library of your mind. On one particular shelf is a set of books that contains your convictions.

They are, in many ways, the basis for your decision-making, rooted in deep-held beliefs central to your essence. What would it look like for you to pull these books off the shelf and start looking into them with a critical eye? Upon deep inspection, poring over these volumes, you will likely find these convictions are based on a startling mixture of fact and fiction.

While many souls never bother to understand their own beliefs, I have learned it is essential for the leader to continually revisit their convictions, especially as they aspire to increasing levels of leadership. There are many deep-rooted convictions in your library, and they must each be evaluated and separated between fact and fiction. The reality is, until you go through this effort, you really have no level of certainty about what is driving your decision-making. This should alarm you as a leader who is responsible for guiding and directing the lives of an entire organization.

What does it look like practically to start this process? Well, first, you might need some help identifying your own convictions. Your friends and closest peers are often a good place to start. Usually, they can tell you a lot about yourself without much hesitation. They know whether family is more important to you than money, they know whether you have a low tolerance for incompetence, or whether you have a long-suffering heart.

As an example, let's say you hold a deep-held belief you are the maker of your own destiny. It's a common conviction for many, but is it true? Depending on your answer, your leadership will take a vastly different approach. You will either build an organization centered on individual performers or one rooted in the power of the team. You will also find your ability to mentor and hold individuals accountable will largely depend on your convictions about individual agency.

This may seem like a small thing, but it is very profound. You will find yourself and your organization running up against barriers to growth, and struggle to understand why it keeps happening. Very often, a deep-held conviction driving your decision-making is preventing the organization from moving forward on the right path. This activity of diving into our own minds and souls to evaluate the condition of our hearts is called the process of maturity.

There is an important truth for the leader to understand: Maturity is not an option. You must continue to break apart and evaluate all areas of your life and be willing to be rebuilt in the service of the organization. Keep searching, keep asking questions, and be willing to embrace the answers that will grow your leadership.

NOW GO LEAD

<u>FIVE MINUTE REFLECTION</u>

Am I spending enough time reviewing and evaluating the substance of my convictions?
Are there unseen biases affecting my leadership?
What convictions do I hold that may or may not be true?

YOUR TIME IS NOW

Could it be every experience in your life has brought you to this moment?

Everything in your life has led to this moment. Let the thought soak in for a moment. Some of what led you here has required careful, thoughtful planning, and, of course, there are the critical turns in the journey you never could have orchestrated. Whatever the path, your leadership has been shaped by the trials, successes, and failures unique to your story. The question in front of you today is simple: what will you do with the opportunity you have been given in this moment?

Around 480 BC, during the height of the Persian Empire, King Xerxes decided to search the entire realm for a new queen. After evaluating and screening the finest the world had to offer, he chose a Jewish woman named Esther. The Jewish people at the time were living scattered across Assyria, having been forced out of Israel after years of rebelling against the former Babylonian Empire. While the Persian Empire generally allowed religious freedom, Esther was careful to keep her faith out of the empire's political spotlight. Even still, Esther was raised very much immersed in her Jewish faith, having been raised by her uncle, Mordecai.

Shortly after Esther's ascension to the throne, Mordecai found himself in conflict with one of Xerxes's advisors, who wielded considerable influence in the empire and with the king. This advisor, Haman, became so furious with Mordecai he devised a plan to have him killed. Using his influence, Haman tricked the king into signing an edict calling for the complete genocide of every Jewish person in the empire. When

Mordecai learned of the plot, he sent a warning to the queen and urged her to intercede with the king on behalf of her people.

Esther was initially reluctant to approach the king. Not only would she have to reveal her hidden heritage, but simply approaching the king uninvited was also an act that could mean her death. Still, Mordecai persisted, and he delivered a line that still resonates with me every time I read it:

"For if you remain silent at this time, relief and deliverance for the Jews will arise from another place, but you and your father's family will perish. And who knows but that you have come to your royal position for such a time as this?"[1]

Mordecai understood something several hundred years ago that still holds true for you today: **Everything in your life has led to this moment, and now it is your time to lead.** The question is whether you can recognize this moment and whether you will have the courage to do what needs to be done? The words, the musings, and the teachings in this book are designed to level up your leadership, but I cannot be the one to act on your behalf. **You** must be the one to do what no one else is willing to do.

When I look back at my own journey, I remember the moments when the opportunity came for me to rise to the occasion. These moments are very rarely born out of ideal circumstances but rather are brought about during seasons of extreme difficulty and uncertainty. I have marveled at how individuals with loads of bravado during high times are often the most absent during times of difficulty. There are truly only a few brave souls with the grit to continue leading in the darkest of moments.

It's definitely much more peaceful to sit back in the relative peace of the royal palace, but I know that the heart of the true leader yearns to be free from complacency. If you turn away now, will you spend the rest of your life wondering what could have been? Sometimes the joy of success lies just beyond the fear of taking the first step.

Sure, it's much more peaceful to sit back in the relative peace of the royal palace, but I know that the heart of the true leader yearns to be free from complacency. If you turn away now, will you spend the rest of

---

your life wondering what could've been? Sometimes the joy of success lies just beyond the fear of taking the first step.

NOW GO LEAD

<u>FIVE MINUTE REFLECTION</u>

Have I come into this place in my life for such a time as this?

THE RECOVERY

Are you recovering?

You might not know it by looking at me, but there was a time in my life when I really got into weightlifting. It started back in high school when I had to find something to do during the off-season athletics. While I never had the size or weight to compete in football, I discovered weightlifting gave me a competitive outlet without being required to weigh more than a water buffalo. As with most things in my life, I dove into the deep end and tried to learn everything I could about how to succeed. One of the best books I bought was the *Modern Encyclopedia of Modern Bodybuilding* by Arnold Schwarzenegger.

In his book, Arnold covers everything about bodybuilding, from basic muscle groups to what to wear during a competition. One of my early beliefs about weightlifting was the idea that success depended on the number of reps and hours spent in the weight room. I was surprised to learn how recovery time played such a critical role in muscular development. Effectively, muscle growth happens not in the weight room, but while you are resting and recovering at home. Lifting weights actually breaks down muscles. The recovery process is where gains are realized.

Whether you are aware of it or not, your leadership journey is wearing you down. Every day you carry the burden and move the organization forward, the demands of leadership are exacting a toll on your heart, body, and soul. The solution is not to spend more time in the office, answer more emails, or work over the occasional weekend. These extra efforts will break you down further, and you may eventually find yourself in a place where you can no longer perform the functions of basic leadership. The answer to growing your leadership is to be intentional about how you spend your time in recovery.

Recovery is an essential activity for a healthy leader, and the amount of recovery required is directly correlated with the demands of your leadership journey. Healthy recovery time has two critical components: it must be intentional and it must be protected. Exactly what you do during your recovery time is at your discretion, but it should include activities specifically focused on allowing your heart and soul to be nourished back to health. Recovery for me is usually done in solitude, and I intentionally include a mix of sleep, reading, and "mindless" entertainment like video games and movies. Whatever you choose to do, be intentional about weekly recovery and protect the time with vigilance.

If you haven't already, your next task is to open your calendar and schedule time for leadership recovery. Find the activities that replenish your reserves and allow yourself the time to recover. A fresh heart and mind equip you to return and lead well.

NOW GO LEAD

FIVE MINUTE REFLECTION

Am I trying to grow my leadership by just working harder, or have I built in the necessary recovery time to realize true leadership gains?

HAPPY IS OK

Are you afraid to be happy?

At some point in my leadership journey, I developed a unique condition: a fear of being happy. It almost felt that if I allowed myself to experience a moment of happiness or joy, I was also choosing not to think about the problems, issues, and organizational fires that needed my attention. No one else carried the responsibility for the organization's constant stream of issues, and I feared laying them down, even briefly, because I wasn't sure I would be able or willing to take them up again.

Since many of the leader's tasks are often difficult, the leader is familiar with sadness, hopelessness, and sorrow as part of the normal course of the journey. Consequently, some leaders often feel guilty when they are happy because it feels like they are not doing their job or not focusing on the task at hand. I am consistently reminded of the verse from Proverbs:

"A little sleep, a little slumber, a little folding of the hands to rest, and poverty will come on you like a thief and scarcity like an armed man."[1]

Because I had developed an unhealthy association between happiness and the dereliction of leadership duty, I also felt being happy meant I wasn't working hard enough to fight poverty and scarcity. I really wish I could go back and ask the person who wrote the proverb how much "a little" really means. Is it five minutes? Is it a week? We may never know.

But in all honesty, I have found that as I get older, it is increasingly challenging for me to allow myself to be happy. I know I am not alone

---

1   Proverbs 6:10-11

in this sentiment, based on the many conversations I have had with other organizational leaders.

Why do we feel this way? First, we need to understand that happiness, just like any other emotion, is a healthy expression of the desires in our hearts. Not allowing ourselves to experience the emotions that well up deep within us can have a catastrophic effect on our long-term health. Happiness is an essential emotion for the leader, as it brings lucid moments of relief and often a reset of perspective. Happiness is a refreshing emotion which can carry the leader through challenging moments. It certainly shouldn't make us feel guilty.

Leader, you are also human. The world didn't start with you, and it will go on after you are gone. Taking up the burdens of leadership may be your lot in life, but happiness is a gift as well, and you should not ignore the blessed moments of respite that come from accepting it freely.

NOW GO LEAD

FIVE MINUTE REFLECTION

Am I uncomfortable with the emotion of happiness?
What lies do I need to break down so I can leverage the healthy emotion of happiness in my life?

THE DANGEROUS LOOKBACK

Are you enjoying your life right now?

Think about it. Leadership has stretches that feel heavy, anxious, and exhausting, so it becomes important to notice the beauty emerging along the way. There are moments in life where your spirit feels full, your relationships are solid, and your career or business is thriving, and your passion for life returns. Together, these experiences create a sense of bliss when life is just what it is supposed to be. There is a deep longing in our souls that awakens when we experience these moments. It is a primal, innate desire, and I know you understand what I'm talking about if you've been on this journey long enough.

But just like anything else in life, we taste something good and then seek to fill the entire existence of our life with the feeling. You find yourself in the "ideal" set of circumstances, and you begin to put down roots and establish boundaries to protect the paradise you've found. Unfortunately, there are several problems with this course of action. Mainly, you begin exerting some control over your relationships to keep them from falling apart. Secondly, you start to avoid paths forward for growth that could have a lasting impact on your leadership journey.

There is a story in Genesis about a man named Lot. A brief background: as a young man, Lot had traveled from a foreign land and established a good life for himself and his family in a beautiful and fertile location near the Jordan River. *Lot's life was really good.*

A while later, God came to Lot and told him it was time to leave because some unsavory activities were happening in Lot's hometown, and God was planning to destroy the whole city with fire. Before destroying the city, God gave Lot and his family a head start and told them specifically, *"Don't look back."* As the story goes, Lot and his family escaped the city and were well on their way to safety when his wife looked back, despite the clear warning not to. With one brief glance back, her life came to an abrupt end.

Let me circle back for a minute and say this clearly: if you're in one of those peaceful, joy-filled seasons of life, slow down and soak it in. Don't rush past the goodness. However if you're starting to sense it's time to move on — if something inside you keeps nudging you forward — then you already know what you need to do. You'll have to make the hard call to turn the page and step into the next stretch of the journey.

Now here's what really gets me about this story — and I want you to lean in for this part. God wasn't trying to wipe out Lot's entire life, burn down everything he cared about, or destroy his future. The judgment was aimed at the cities soaked in corruption, not at the man God was pulling out of the mess.

But in the middle of all this destruction, everything familiar to Lot still disappeared. His home...gone. His community...gone. The life he had built...gone. The whole scene was total devastation — in modern terms, it was basically nuclear. **Are you getting this?**

The point wasn't annihilation, it was separation. God was rescuing Lot by cutting him loose from an environment quietly destroying him. The fire wasn't meant for Lot, but it burned away every tether keeping him tied to a place he was never meant to stay.

Honestly, leadership feels like this sometimes. There are seasons when everything you counted on collapses. You lose people, systems break down, the familiar disappears, and you're left wondering what happened. But sometimes the only path forward is the one where the old structures have to burn away so you can finally move toward the life you are meant to lead. The real question becomes: *will you keep walking, or will you look back*?

There is also another trap for leaders to avoid. If you are courageous enough to lead your team out of your comfort zone and into the unknown future, you must be committed to not looking back. The leader that is constantly looking back cannot possibly see the way forward. Their soul will get so lost in regret or in wishing for better days from the past, that they can't see what needs to be done to move the organization forward.

Today, I urge you to face the road ahead and not look back at regret or mistakes. I can assure you there will be more moments of bliss along the journey, but when it is time to leave the past behind, you must be willing to lead the organization forward. Otherwise, you risk ending the journey early and missing out on the opportunity to grow your leadership.

NOW GO LEAD

FIVE MINUTE REFLECTION

In what ways am I trying to control my relationships and circumstances because I'm afraid to move forward?
Am I putting my entire organization at risk by holding them back instead of leading them forward?
What regret from my past do I need to let go of in order to face the future and move forward?

DON'T BOW DOWN

What are your non-negotiables?

Sometimes when I am writing about leadership, it feels like I'm talking out of both sides of my mouth. We talk about staying focused, and then we turn around and talk about taking time off to rest. We talk about staying true to who we are and then we drive home the necessity of change and growth. What emerges in the leadership journey is actually a bit of a balancing act. You will have to continually try to see both sides of every issue and you'll be forced, sometimes reluctantly, to change some long-standing beliefs that are hard to break away from. We've talked before about the process of evaluating our leadership convictions, and even though it is an activity most leaders don't tackle until later in the journey, it becomes increasingly necessary as the stakes grow.

During the Israelite exile in Babylon, the king selected some of the Jewish people's most capable individuals and trained them to hold leadership positions in the empire. These individuals had high distinction in the empire and were well regarded for their intelligence and wisdom. At some point later in their leadership journey, they encountered a situation destined to test the very grit of their souls. The king had recently issued new edicts requiring compulsory worship of a golden statue or facing the death sentence. This was not necessarily a big deal for most of the people in the empire, but for a Jew, this was tantamount to the most serious transgressions one could commit. The story reached a crisis of belief when the king decided to hold a public spectacle in which everyone present, including his leadership team, would be required to bow before his shiny golden statue.

There will be times in your leadership journey when your values will be put to the test on a very public and open platform. These pressures are particularly strong when there is an obvious, easy solution to move the ball forward but would compromise your core values. I look back at those young leaders standing with the king, waiting for the order to come for everyone to bow down. Were their hearts torn? Certainly, no one would blame them for following the crowd. I wonder if there were other Israelites out in the crowd who recognized them and were watching to see what they would do. As the story reaches its climax, it is revealed that the small group of leaders had already decided in their hearts what they would do: **they would not bow down.** Independent of what consequences would ensue, they made up their minds to hold true to what they believed.

You may have already done the hard work of getting your core values and convictions lined out. However, if you are constantly vacillating between compromise and purity, you might need to spend some time strengthening your resolve. As Proverbs says, "If you fall to pieces in a crisis, there wasn't much to you in the first place."

Today, settle the non-negotiables for your leadership journey. You don't want to be making these decisions under the inevitable pressure you will face when a crisis strikes. If you settle this now, you will be much better prepared to adapt since the difficult questions have already been answered.[1]

NOW GO LEAD

---

1   Proverbs 24:10 MSG

FIVE MINUTE REFLECTION

Do I have the important issues in my life and
leadership settled?
Where am I willing to compromise, and what things
are non-negotiable?

POWERFUL LEADERSHIP

Do you understand the power of leadership?

I was recently walking on the shores of the Niagara River in New York. The National Park is open 24 hours a day, so I arrived early in the morning ahead of the daily crowds. As I walked along, I noticed how the water starts off relatively calm as it empties from Lake Erie, but as it winds toward the inevitable falls, the water's power manifests in relentless whitecaps and terrifying currents. It's astounding how much power develops when something as commonplace as water is given focus and purpose as the channel tightens and unstoppable momentum takes over.

It's sometimes easy for a developing leader to see their skills as commonplace and ineffectual. A leader may have tremendous depth and tons of potential, but without focus and a destination, they never really produce anything remarkable. Whether you realize it or not, you have tremendous potential developing just beneath the surface. However, the manifestation of your power will never emerge if you are not able to bring focus and vision to your leadership journey.

The first step in realizing your greatest potential is to commit to an irreversible path. Another way to put this is to go "all-in" on the journey. To be fair, this is a big step, and one many will never take. The open waters of Lake Easy are comfortable, and there is not too much effort required to navigate the occasional breeze that may push you along. You may not be making any real progress, but there is also very little required to stay afloat. However, the commitment to exit the lake means you've decided to narrow your focus and test your mettle against a much greater challenge. It also means you are ready to see the real power of your leadership.

The rapids of true leadership will put all your skills to the test, and you will be stretched in heart, mind, and soul as you struggle to survive. However, as you gain strength and experience along the journey, you soon notice how much more capable you've become in facing the rising challenges of advanced leadership. The skills that once seemed ineffectual and useless have now grown and allowed you to become an influential leader capable of amazing things. Your mental strength and courage of heart have now prepared you to take on even the most difficult parts of the journey.

Momentum created by powerful leadership is hard to stop, and its energy will ripple through the organization. Teams fueled by this momentum are more prepared and agile than their competitors. They are the organizations leaning into the journey and are always looking ahead to the next big challenge. Today, commit to unleashing your full leadership potential. You may need to make some significant changes and address decisions you've been delaying. The rapids are calling you; will you answer?

NOW GO LEAD

FIVE MINUTE REFLECTION

What is holding me back from advancing to the highest
levels of leadership?

Has my organizational momentum slowed because the
leadership at the top lacks force, clarity, or conviction?

MALK AND FRIED CHICKEN

Can I offer you a substitute?

We are out of milk. I just put oat Malk in my coffee this morning. That's not a misspelling; it's a real thing. It's a substitute for real milk, so not even the real thing. But I put it in my coffee this morning, and I'm sitting here mourning the loss of that genuine dairy-filled brew I can never get back. I am suddenly aware we live in a world filled with options and alternatives. Some are designed to suit our individual preferences; others can meet specific needs. There are also the knockoffs claiming to offer all the benefits of the genuine article at a reduced price or perhaps solve some trendy problem we didn't even know we needed to solve until it showed up on social media. I distinctly remember growing up in a world where we had two types of milk in the store: the one with the red cap and the one with the green cap. That was it, there was no oat milk, almond milk, soy milk, nut pods, etc. Now I have two gallons of the alternative in my fridge.

Along your journey, you will be asked to modify and expand your leadership offerings to your organization. This expectation is reasonable at some level because within your ever-expanding sphere of influence, you will find wide varieties of needs and challenges that don't meet the "one size fits all" criteria. However if you spread your leadership offering too thin, you risk diluting your brand and letting compromises creep in that take you far from your leadership philosophy and away from the vision.

On the periphery, I am aware of cable channels like Hallmark and Lifetime. I don't watch them, but I have friends (male and female) who love the programming, particularly the Holiday movies that start right after Halloween and run through the New Year. According to Lifetime, their channel "is committed to offering the highest quality entertainment and information programming." That sounds like a noble endeavor, right? Well, back in 2018, the geniuses responsible for developing programs for Lifetime decided to produce a short film called *A Recipe for Seduction* starring Mario Lopez as Colonel Sanders (the founder and mascot of KFC). This travesty of "high quality entertainment" is basically AC Slater wearing a Fu Manchu beard and selling fried chicken. It is bizarre to say the least, and I can't help but wonder, *"How did this happen?"* I can't imagine Colonel Sanders had it in his original vision to create B-roll romantic comedies for channel 300 on cable, and I can't believe the founders of Lifetime wanted to fill airtime with hour-long chicken commercials.

The leadership path you walk toward the vision should narrow as you advance. If you reach a place where you are trying to be all things, you will begin to produce mediocrity instead of excellence. Don't fall into the temptation to make compromises or offer cheap substitutes to your leadership brand. Integrity in leadership is sacred, and you must fight the urge to dilute your brand with cheap substitutes and compromised values.

I hope at the end of your journey you're not sitting at a table with a cup of Malk and a bucket of fried chicken when you could have had so much more. Today, commit to following your vision for leadership with a dogged pursuit of authenticity and making no compromises along the way.

NOW GO LEAD

FIVE MINUTE REFLECTION

Have I let my organization down by not acknowledging and addressing my leadership weaknesses?
Who do I need to elevate or bring into my circle of trust to protect the organization from unnecessary risk?

TREAT YOURSELF

How do you treat yourself?

You may have one person following you, or hundreds. You have a responsibility to treat them well. This almost feels trite, but it is true. The fact that I have to say it out loud might indicate to you that many leaders, for whatever reason, don't treat their people well. I used to think this was related to leadership immaturity, and simply pointing out the obvious shortcomings would fix the problem. But then another issue would pop up, then another, then another. It took me some time to see the clear connections between how a leader treats themselves and how they treat their organization.

I was late to the party, but *Parks and Recreation* has become one of my all-time favorite sitcoms. Plenty of the characters on the show are selfish, but perhaps none more self-absorbed than Tom Haverford. Tom has a panache for all things style. He constantly celebrates and exalts himself, all to a comedic effect, giving him a certain undeniable pathos. One of the funnier episodes revolves around Tom's special day of the year, called "Treat Yourself". On this special day, Tom will team up with his co-worker, Donna, and they will shower themselves with indulgent gifts and services beyond absurdity. If you follow the character of Tom throughout the series, you will see he not only treats himself well, but also gives extravagantly to those closest to him. It's all meant to serve up laughs, but it caused me to think about a deeper spiritual truth: our command to treat others as we treat ourselves.

When Jesus tells his followers to love others as themselves, we understand it to mean we should treat our neighbors kindly and with the same grace we give ourselves every day. But let's step back for a minute and consider how we treat ourselves as leaders. One of the hardest lessons I had to learn as a leader is, in so many ways, people don't want to be treated the way I treat myself. I am super hard on myself and generally unforgiving. I have trouble letting go of small things, and I have big expectations. I push myself to grow and continually sacrifice myself, my friends, and my family for the greater good. I don't give myself enough time off work, and I tell myself everything will fall apart if I fail. I mean, who would want to follow anyone under those expectations? I had to learn to treat myself well before I could lead others well.

Treating yourself well as a leader is the first step towards being a person who can truly care well for others. Contrary to Tom's idea of "Treat Yourself", this doesn't mean spending your hard-earned money on absurdities and trivial pursuits. In fact, this could backfire on you if your organization starts to see you as self-indulgent. Instead you need to indulge in the graces offered to you in this life from God, your family, and your friends. The expectations you have for yourself are likely none but yours. They originated in your brain, and you perpetuate them every day in a vain effort to persecute yourself into success. Do you ever wonder why some leaders struggle to keep close friends? They are just treating their friends the way they treat themselves! It's time to stop the insanity and start leading our own lives with the respect and dignity we know we want to share with others.

Today, commit to treating yourself the way you want others to treat you. Give yourself the margin to grow, the grace to fail, and set the bar low enough to realize success. When you learn the discipline to treat yourself well, you will become the leader organizations love to follow: a leader who loves themselves just like they love others.

NOW GO LEAD

FIVE MINUTE REFLECTION

How am I treating myself?
If I take an honest look at the pressures and expectations I place on my own shoulders, would my organization say I treat them the same way? Are those expectations fair and reasonable, or am I projecting my own impossible standard of perfection onto people who don't deserve to carry it?

VERMONT

How do you recover?

The first half of one particular year was utterly hellish for me. It started off with a bad three months of business invoicing and revenue, which led to some unwelcome staff reductions. The economic uncertainty had a negative ripple throughout the organization, and several other people ended up leaving, which we really couldn't afford to lose. One of my senior leaders unexpectedly resigned. Another close friend informed me their marriage was falling apart and they needed to take some extended time off. I had yet another senior leader who I had allowed to transition to a four-day work week the year prior as they were winding down towards retirement. I had to ask them to step in and cover some essential tasks temporarily while we built up enough cash to hire more help, which didn't go over too well. My business partner took a scheduled, but inconveniently timed, mission trip and had to take an extra week on the back end to recover from COVID. By the time July rolled around, I was completely fried — fried like a piece of bacon left in the skillet too long. I was ready to break into pieces with just a little snap. I had spent all my reserves, and no one really cared, because I was doing my job.

After the July 4th holiday I decided to take some extended time off in August. Typically, I would give myself and my organization much more time to prepare for a four-week vacation, but I felt like Rocky after fourteen rounds with Apollo. I was sucking wind, I looked terrible, and I was about to hit the mat hard. I found myself browsing vacation rentals in Vermont, and I came across something that just called to my soul. It was a small one-room cabin sitting just off the banks of a clear-water pond. I booked it immediately. The intermittent weeks leading up to my time off were filled with visions of Golden Pond and sweet isolation. I was in the middle of writing my first book, and I could see myself enveloped in endless inspiration, making significant progress. Finally, after a twenty-two-hour drive from Arkansas, I arrived and took a deep breath. Peace at last.

It took me all of ten minutes to unpack my meager provisions. I took a quick lap around the pond and then sat down in the cabin to be still for a moment. And then it hit me. My brain immediately pushed me to start reaching for my phone. I was painfully aware of the lack of television. I was at least a mile from the nearest living soul. How was I going to survive being alone and cut off from media for an entire week? I didn't even have air conditioning! I did the only thing I could think of doing: I fell asleep. After a nice 12 hours of sleep, I figured I would be ready to write. I opened my laptop, but nothing happened. My soul was giving me nothing. I started to panic because I knew I would have limited time to be alone and away from the day-to-day. I calmed myself and decided instead to pick up a book and read. After about an hour, I put the book down and just walked out onto the front porch of the cabin. It was stunningly beautiful. Right then, I made a decision that would change the trajectory of my entire vacation: instead of trying to force my soul to respond, I decided to listen to it instead.

I spent the rest of my time in Vermont just letting my soul lead. My brain, on the other hand, fought hard to get its fix of accomplishment, a clean inbox, and a few texts sent. It was a battle initially, but eventually, there was a comforting calm as the anxiety gave way to peace. I got bored, and it was absolutely wonderful. After a week at the cabin, I had accomplished almost nothing of note. I packed up my things and made the drive back to Arkansas, feeling lighter than I had in years. The solitude and intentional boredom did more for my soul than any amount of accomplishment could ever provide. I started thinking about leadership.

Leadership expectations are often too high. When I told people about my time in Vermont, most were a little nonplussed and almost sad that I hadn't written the next great book on leadership or achieved some new, powerful vision for the future of our organization. However, I did learn an important truth about recovery during the leadership process. ***Sometimes the leader just needs to stop.*** Stop striving, stop achieving, stop trying to have the most awesome vacation, stop trying to lead every single thing in their lives. This was hard for me. I'm used to the high expectations at work, but I was amazed at how much of it carried over into my time off. I brought the same expectations for myself from work right into vacation, but that was exactly the thing I needed to get away from.

You are probably doing this at some level too: trying to create monumental experiences out of every banal part of your life. You want the interior of your house to be ready for that surprise visit from Joanna Gaines; you want your wardrobe to be trendy; you spend absurd hours keeping up with the latest fleeting social trends, music, and streaming series. You are trying to raise perfect kids, build a healthy retirement portfolio, and keep the lawn looking better than your neighbor's derelict property. What you are really doing is killing the soul of what really makes you a leader.

Real recovery for the soul is not going to happen simply because you are away from your desk or work environment. You could take six months off work or relocate across the country, but until you lay down the unrealistic expectations you are carrying, your soul cannot be nourished. Put the brakes on your brain when you get home at night. Stop filling it with an endless list of projects, self-improvements, playlists, and once-in-a-lifetime getaway experiences. You don't need any of that to restore your soul; you need to stop and listen.

NOW GO LEAD

<u>FIVE MINUTE REFLECTION</u>

How can I create some margin in my life for true stillness and solitude?

Am I pushing myself to succeed in all parts of my life while my soul is slowly starving to death?

How would it feel to just be still and not have any expectations for a portion of my day?

SCREW IT

Aren't leadership screw ups the worst?

Countless lives depend on competent leadership every day. People have put their trust in you to lead them safely towards the goal by taking them on the right path and protecting them from many traps along the way. Your strength is their greatest comfort. Leadership strengths are great. However, it is your weaknesses you should be concerned about. The areas of your leadership where you are the weakest are exactly where your organization is most vulnerable.

As an engineer, I have great admiration for people like Thomas Edison and Henry Ford. At some level or another, their leadership and hard work are responsible for the lives we are able to live today. When Henry Ford invented a cheap and effective way to mass-produce automobiles, it changed everything. Being first to market mass-produced automobiles meant great things for the Ford organization. During the early 1900s, Henry Ford became one of the wealthiest people to ever live. His tenacity, genius, and hard work, all combined with a powerful vision, created a symphony of magic. But like many leaders, Henry had a weakness; his was pride. When competition ramped up from competitors like General Motors in the 1920s, Ford's advisors encouraged him to start making changes to their aging model line. Sure, it would mean an expensive overhaul to his venerable assembly line, but Ford believed the real problem was poor performance from the sales staff. The car was fine. Ford was fine. There was no need to run out and do anything rash and expensive. Years later, by the end of the Second World War, Ford was on the edge of bankruptcy.

Obviously, even great leaders can screw up sometimes. We are all just men and women trying to accomplish something great in this world, but we all have our flaws. However, the greatest leaders are not only aware of their weaknesses but take measures to ensure their personal weaknesses don't expose the organization to unnecessary risk. If you are unaware of your weaknesses, you may be leading with a blind spot, which means your flanks are exposed, and you may not be able to see the danger coming up behind you. On the other hand, you may be keenly aware of your weaknesses, and you might not be quite sure how to compensate. You really have a couple of options, depending on the size of your organization. Long term, you need to bring in someone to balance your deficiencies, someone whose strength is more than an equal match for your shortcomings. Fair warning: there will be an adjustment period for your organization when you bring in someone who will challenge your latent leadership qualities. You'll need the humility to accept constructive feedback and learn to trust your new advisor. Eventually, though, this will be a recipe for sustainable organizational growth.

Screw ups on the part of the leader are going to happen. However, they don't have to be repeated. The very best leaders will learn to recover from failure, strengthen the organization, and prevent their weaknesses from becoming long-term liabilities.

NOW GO LEAD

FIVE MINUTE REFLECTION

Have I let my organization down by not acknowledging and
addressing my leadership weaknesses?
Who do I need to elevate or bring into my circle of trust to protect
the organization from unnecessary risk?

THE MAJOR

How's your little fief?

Have you ever seen anyone completely out of their element? I hope you are surrounded by a team of competent business leaders who can confidently take on problems that would leave most people cowering in the corner, but if you took the same group of people out to a dance club, you might be in for a bona fide cringe fest. How does the same leader who is so resplendent in a boardroom suddenly become a prancing pariah when they step under a disco ball? The truth is we are leaders of habit, and we seek to remain in environments that are both familiar and comforting places for us to grow our leadership, but when does comfort and familiarity become a barrier to organizational growth?

We put it off for a long time, but just before the 2020 pandemic, we decided to adopt a pet. The kids were old enough to share the responsibility, and we felt like it wouldn't be too disruptive to our schedule. On a Saturday morning, I took the girls out to a feline adoption event, and we brought home our first family pet, Major. Major is a great cat; he is patient with my children's suffocating hugs and routinely grabs a seat at the table with us for dinner. He spends more time in the house than any other family member, so, in some sense, he rules the house. He goes where he pleases, sleeps and eats whenever he wants, and occasionally will grace an empty lap with his regalness.

It wasn't until about two years after we adopted him when Major began to be aware there was a world outside the confines of our house. Aware in the sense that he began to understand the thresholds these humans passed through every day were actually portals to an unknown realm. I could tell he was interested because he would follow me right up to the door and then stop at this invisible barrier. I decided one day to pick him up and walk outside with him. He became a completely different animal. The once confident and secure Major became a noodle-spined flurry of fur and claws that I could barely contain. He scampered back into the house, and I headed for the first aid kit.

In the subsequent years, Major has found a nice comfortable little life within the walls of our house. He struggles with his weight, and I'm certain part of his soul longs for the wild and a place to find fulfillment for his feral instincts. But he has chosen, or perhaps defaulted, to the life of problem-free predictability.

It's not my place to decide the trajectory of your leadership journey. Some of you will have higher aspirations than others. There is no "right" path, and there seems to be a place for everyone to choose their own adventure. I also know there are leaders out there who long for more. They are sitting at their desk, looking out over their fiefdom and wondering, "Is this all there is?" The answer really depends on you. What are you willing to sacrifice? Will you give up your comforts? Are you willing to risk failure and to bring your organization along on that journey? Would you rather settle for being fat and happy?

I hope you are at least willing to consider what a greater calling might look like for your leadership journey. The greatest leaders have been those willing to risk comfort and security for the pursuit of a vision beyond their ability to predict the outcome. There is a world out there calling for leaders who will go and lead.

NOW GO LEAD

<u>FIVE MINUTE REFLECTION</u>

What do I want from my leadership journey?
Have I let fear hold me back from stepping into the unknown?
Do I need to let go of pretension and ego and take the risk to pursue
a greater calling?

MY FAVORITE BAR

Where do you go?

Sometimes you want to be in a place where everyone knows your name. A leader's motivations can be misunderstood, and their decisions are constantly being criticized or second-guessed. Leading is a lonely activity most of the time, and within the confines of the organization, you'll find very few people have the capacity to comprehend all the leadership activities required to keep the organization progressing toward the vision.

Back in 1981, a songwriter named Gary Portnoy was asked to partner with Judy Hart to come up with some compositions for a new musical. The outcome was a number called "People Like Us". Although the musical never garnered much attention, one of the songs later found its way into the hands of a TV producer who thought it would be a good fit for an upcoming sitcom. Portnoy reworked the lyrics to what would eventually become the theme for Cheers. If you don't know, Cheers was a sitcom about a bar where people gathered to commiserate about the ills common to life. I loved the sitcom as a kid, but the words in the opening theme resonate in my heart as an adult today:

Makin' your way in the world today takes everything you've got.
Takin' a break from all your worries sure would help a lot.
Wouldn't you like to get away?[1]

---

1 Gary Portnoy. (n.d.). The Cheers story | Cheers theme song. Gary-Portnoy.com.

As a new and growing leader, you may not understand this need and longing until you begin to experience periods of loneliness on the journey.

I've had the privilege of receiving counsel from a wise human resources professional at my company. Once, during one of our regular meetings, she encouraged me to "go be with my people." What she was telling me to do was go and find a place where I could be with people who knew and understood my struggles as a leader.

There are quite a few options available to leaders depending on their location, money, and bandwidth. I ended up connecting with a national peer group which became a safe place that didn't exist within my own organization. It became a place where I could let my guard down, vent, and openly discuss problems without fear of retribution and overreaction. It became my favorite bar.

Don't ignore the potential benefit and warmth that can come from a great peer group where you can share your leadership troubles. *It really does help a lot.* Your organization will share in the benefits of your investment in taking time away to gain from and give to other leaders who are out pursuing their own vision. Take a leadership cue from me and find your favorite bar. Wouldn't you like to get away?

NOW GO LEAD

FIVE MINUTE REFLECTION

Do I have a place where I can be a person instead of a leader?
Who are the people outside my organization who understand me
and are willing to help me process the difficulties of pursuing the
vision without fear of retribution or shame?

CARMINE SIXES

Is it really about the shoes?

What would happen to your leadership if you were suddenly stripped of your title or fired from your job? Would those in your sphere of influence suddenly disappear? I wonder about this a lot. I have been running my own company for nearly 20 years, and to some extent, my sphere of influence has grown purely as a function of the growth of our business. I have people who look to my leadership (good or bad) simply because I have the prerogatives reserved for the company's founder. I have tried my hardest to live up to these expectations and earn the right to lead, yet I can't help but wonder in my heart sometimes whether my leadership is authentic. Maybe you've been there too.

Back in 1991, shopping malls were very much the retail manifestation of popular culture. If there was something advertised on TV or discussed in the lunchroom at school, the mall was the place to get it. Consequently, I found the mall to be a particularly attractive destination for my thirteen-year-old self. I lived in a rural part of the country, so when we did get out to the mall, it was always a memorable experience. It was about this time in my life when I noticed what people were wearing to school and developed my own ideas of style. During a trip to the mall that same year I fell in love for the first time. It was a chance meeting as I was walking by Foot Locker, and I was caught dead in my tracks at the beauty before me: Carmine Red Air Jordans.

I don't believe I have ever wanted something more in my entire life. These shoes would make me whole. I would find new meaning in my own life, not to mention the elevated status I would certainly gain among my peers. I began to think about the conversations I would have;

people who previously didn't care about my existence would suddenly be drawn to the exquisite shoes adorning my feet. Doors would be opened. There was even an outside chance that some of Michael Jordan's magic might transfer to my own body, and I would be the only sixth grader in America who could dunk a basketball. Of course, there was one small problem.

I picked up the sneaker from the display shelf, and my heart sank a little: $125 a pair. That's roughly $300 in today's currency. Even as a parent today, I would have a really hard time buying a pair of sneakers at that price for my kids, knowing they'll be outgrown in a short matter of months. But Nike is no slouch when it comes to business. They released these shoes in November, which meant there was an opportunity for most kids that wouldn't exist any other time of the year: Christmas. I knew what Nike knew. If I played my cards right, I could bag a new pair of sneakers way out of my normal price range. It would only be a week or so later when I got the requisite "What do you want for Christmas this year?" from my parents. I was intoxicated with glee and avarice when we went into Foot Locker after Thanksgiving to try on the shoes. Mom wrote the check, and we walked out the door with my shoes. Now it was just a matter of waiting four weeks until Christmas.

Something tragic happened at school the following Monday. I had a friend at school who was the progeny of a local business owner, which meant he had a little more money than the rest of us. I happened to be telling him about the new shoes I had acquired over the weekend when he pulled a brand-new pair of Carmine Jordans out of his gym bag. Oof. I remember distinctly when he teased me about how I would have to wait until Christmas to get my shoes. Of course, his family could afford to get him the shoes at any time. I looked down at my own frayed pair of British Knights (still cool but waning), and suddenly my feet began to ache.

I came home with an ingenious plan. My old shoes were hurting my feet. The answer was practical, obvious, and, if I must say so, quite brilliant. Why not go ahead and start wearing the new shoes now? I wouldn't be asking for anything else at Christmas; I just wanted my feet to stop hurting. There was of course, the side benefit of showing everyone I could have cool things even when it wasn't a special holiday. My carping to mom and dad was initially received with sympathy, but they eventually saw through the ruse. There was no way I was going to get those shoes early.

Still, I persisted, and eventually the dam broke. Mom marched me into the local discount store and told me to find a new pair of shoes. I was amazed at how swiftly my languishing foot problems seemed to vanish like pumpkin spice lattes in September. "Mom, I think I could make these work a little while longer." No dice. We left with a pair of sneakers that cost less than $20, and I was going to have to wear them to school for four weeks. Oh, the humanity.

I was painfully aware of every glance cast down towards my shoes as I walked through the halls of school the next few weeks. It felt as though the entirety of my existence was being perpetrated upon my choice of footwear. There was something very true about the thirteen-year-old version of myself which is true for so many of us today: **Take out the shoes, and you take out the leader.**

Don't put your confidence in your shoes, your job title, or the framed diploma on your wall. These things can be easily taken away, burned, or faded with time. The substance of your leadership is so much more than what people can see on your social media accounts or the job you may have in this moment. The true leader will free their heart from the prison of what people think and open themselves up to the freedom to pursue the vision with an unfettered heart.

NOW GO LEAD

FIVE MINUTE REFLECTION

What is the real substance of my leadership?
If I were to lose some of the dressings and privileges I currently
have, would I still be the same leader?

ASSETS AND LIABILITIES

What is your greatest asset?

Not just anybody can lead. This was my first thought as I started writing today. It's a wholly different statement than whether someone can be promoted or elected to a position of leadership. There are a lot of posers out there with titles like manager, pastor, or president. They've somehow found their way into a leadership position—whether through being good at their job, organizational convenience, relationship, deceit or sheer luck—but not through intentional leadership development. They are given incredible responsibility but have no real ability to lead. At its simplest definition, a leader must have followers. If no one is willing to follow you, then you aren't a leader, no matter what your title may indicate. There is also the fact that just because people will obey your instructions, doesn't mean you're leading them. People who want to keep their jobs are pretty good at following instructions, even if they have a poser for a boss. So, what makes a leader worth following?

Back in the 1980s, evangelical churches in the United States were experiencing tremendous growth; perhaps none more than those being led by Jimmy Swaggart. Jimmy was an evangelist who started with humble beginnings and grew his ministry into a worldwide enterprise. By 1983, his teachings were being broadcast daily from his Baton Rouge campus on over 250 television stations across the US, reaching the ears of millions of people. By the simple nature of his work (Biblical teaching), Jimmy would address the problems of sin and declining American morals with unapologetic fervor. Television programming in the 1980s was becoming more provocative and salacious, with the likes of Dallas and Knots Landing dominating the ratings. Jimmy regularly railed against the sexual promiscuity portrayed in these shows from the pulpit, condemning not only the programming but the larger impact on America, whose values were being eroded. However there was a storm brewing.

A little over an hour away, in New Orleans, another Pentecostal pastor was experiencing enormous success in growing his ministry. Marvin Gorman was like Jimmy in many ways. Both were born in the poor South in the 1930s, and both married at a young age. They grew up about three hours apart, and by the time they were in their 50s, they had both gained substantial influence on the national stage within evangelical Christendom. In so many ways, along with others like Jim Bakker, they were the voice of the evangelical movement to the world.

It was about this time when Jimmy Swaggart invited Marvin Gorman to his home in New Orleans and accused him of having an extramarital affair. What is not clear is how or why Jimmy came across this information. In retrospect, it might be inferred he wanted more power and influence, and sought it under the guise of doing the right thing. We certainly can't have a man committing adultery behind the scenes and leading a large Christian organization on Sundays, right? **Integrity matters!** Under pressure to come forward or be outed, Marvin eventually acknowledged his affair to the public. His empire unraveled spectacularly, and he was defrocked from the Assemblies of God.

Left with plenty of time on his hands, a bit of boiling anger, and some leftover resources, Marvin engaged some of his family members to see what they could find out about Jimmy Swaggart. It wasn't too much later they hit paydirt when they photographed Jimmy at a hotel with a prostitute. Marvin was quick to reach out to Jimmy and inform him of what he knew, along with an ultimatum to confess or be exposed. Jimmy remained silent, and Marvin took what he had to the overseers of the church. The whole ordeal was so much more salacious than even the juiciest episodes of Dallas. Jimmy's life had, in fact, become the very life he preached against. He lost all credibility, and his ministry came crashing down.

As a leader, integrity is your greatest asset. Unfortunately, it only takes one moment of weakness for it to become your greatest liability. It's hard for a leader to take a stand on something when we are all so painfully aware of our own tendency to fall short of our own vision, yet the vision is above reproach and must remain there. Perfect ideals will always be championed by imperfect people, so the best approach for the leader is to never elevate themselves to the perfect levels of the vision. The leader cannot be the embodiment of the vision; they are simply the steward tasked with shepherding the organization along the journey. Even still, a leader without integrity is hard to follow.

For the leader, maintaining integrity comes down to the fundamental tenet of sacrifice. You must give up more, say "no" more often, and pursue a higher calling. You do all of this without acknowledgement from others or any fanfare or celebration. Instead, you take a knee each evening, thank God that you made it another day, and start working for the battle ahead tomorrow. I'm here with you on this one.

NOW GO LEAD

FIVE MINUTE REFLECTION

Have I elevated myself, along with the vision, to a place where my integrity has become a liability?

What shortcomings do I need to step back and acknowledge so that I can move my organization forward with humility instead of pride?

OLD SALT

What's the best way to learn leadership?

The rules, conduct, and roadmap for effective leadership have been well documented. If you believe the millions of words penned by countless authors over the millennia, one should be able to learn everything about leadership without ever taking a single step towards a vision, without ever leading a team through a crisis, or without ever experiencing the pain of loss and failure. There is a bit of irony in our American culture: we encourage our young adults to spend hundreds of thousands of dollars on a quality education, only to tell them, when they enter the workforce, that they know nothing and the job will be a classroom for real learning. Everyone fresh out of college hates to hear this, and every old employee who has been working a job for many knows it to be true.

My daughters played volleyball in high school. I learned as much as I could about the sport and even got my arms around the hand signals for officiating the matches. Suffice it to say, by the time we sat in the stands for the first game, I was an expert. The games were enjoyable to watch, and I even occasionally volunteered as a line judge.

However I will never forget the first time I was asked to sit at the sideline table and fill out the scorecard. I knew how to score volleyball; I had no idea how to fill out a scorecard in real time. The pace is actually very frenetic. You must document who is serving every point, note every side out and every substitution, keep track of the libero running in on every other play, and make sure the score is accurate *for both teams!* All this happens in a volley that can last between one and twenty seconds. I'd never been more lost or under more pressure at a sporting event in my life. The eyes of all the coaches, players, and parents were on me after every kill to make sure I was keeping up. It really changed my perspective on the game, and I now have a much greater appreciation for the work that goes into officiating.

In the classic *Good Will Hunting*, Sean is a therapist tasked with trying to get through to a young genius named Will Hunting. Will is "wicked smart," mainly based on a life of book learning. He has an uncanny ability to remember everything he reads, and he can harness it into total recall, which he uses largely for personal gain. During their initial sessions, Sean has great difficulty making progress with Will, who seems to have the right answer for everything. Will is even able to feign emotional responses that he believes will convince Sean that he doesn't need therapy, which he believes is a waste of time. One day, while sitting at a park bench, Sean delivers a line to Will that finally pierces the impenetrable armor.

> "... *But you're a genius, Will. No one denies that. No one could possibly understand the depths of you. ... You're an orphan, right? Do you think I'd know the first thing about how hard your life has been, how you feel, who you are because I read Oliver Twist? Does that encapsulate you? ... because you know what? I can't learn anything from you I can't read in some ... book.*"

Here I am writing a book about leadership, telling you that books about leadership and knowledge about leadership are really just cheap imitations for the gauntlet of authentic leadership. But behind every book written is a leader with the scars and wounds to prove their words are written from a heart that has known true battle, known the joy, pain, and heartache of giving the best parts of their life to the journey. **The greatest lessons about leadership were learned before they were ever written.** These lessons, one after the other, have combined together to produce the greatest leaders our world has ever known. Do you understand it? The journey IS the path to and through the greatest leadership lessons. The greatest leaders are made in the mundane of the day-to-day by those who are willing to pick up the burden and move it forward, not by the number of diplomas on their wall. Walk with me on this path; I think you'll like where we are headed.

NOW GO LEAD

FIVE MINUTE REFLECTION

Do you ever feel your leadership being threatened by people who
have read more books and have more degrees than you do?
Have you ever taken a book you just read and leveraged it over
someone without really taking time to step into their shoes and
spend time in the trenches by their side?

EUSTACE

Are you hoping to get what's yours one day?

The leadership journey has long and sometimes insufferable stretches of unglamorous drudgery. The very early stages of the leader can sometimes be the most difficult. It is the time when the vision's freshness and burgeoning enthusiasm prompt the leader to begin their own journey. In the initial stages of the journey, the leader has less prerogative and agency than they would like. Young leaders spend years in the throes of middle management. They long for the greater offices of licensure, where one day they will call the shots and pursue a vision purely their own. A young heart is also one full of self. Time and circumstance have not yet done their mighty work to mold the leader. It is a critical moment when a wise heart can see through the onerous tasks of the day-to-day, but a selfish heart can begin to build up scales of resentment.

In the C.S. Lewis fantasy novel, *The Voyage of the Dawn Treader*, Eustace is a boy who doesn't want to put in the work. He came from a background of some privilege and had a decidedly selfish attitude towards life. Consequently, he always felt like he was getting the raw end of the deal. Whatever the situation, Eustace was getting screwed by someone. Later, on an unexplored island, Eustace wanders off and finds the treasure of a long-dead dragon in a cave. With his newfound wealth, Eustace begins to plot revenge on those who have wronged him. He harbors these thoughts as he drifts off to sleep and wakes up completely transformed into a dragon himself. As a dragon, Eustace begins to realize many of the truths that were so evident to others. Mainly, it was *he* who was the problem, and not everyone else. But the transformation into a dragon was not something easily undone. Fortunately for Eustace, he eventually encounters the lion Aslan, who can help, but the cost will be dear.

I don't know the details of your journey, but if you are reading this, you are probably human, and that means you've got some dragon scales that have formed along the journey. These scales have at times made you feel you have power over other people, but they ultimately keep you from taking your leadership to the next level. You've finally gotten to a place in the journey where things are starting to shake loose, but you are harboring some resentment and anger which is slowly killing the soft part of your heart needing to be open to growth.

Aslan was a kind and compassionate leader who had the exact tools necessary to heal Eustace. However, it was up to Eustace to submit to the painful process of tearing away the scales of selfishness he had allowed to develop. The process was painful, but ultimately Eustace became whole again and, in no small way, became who he was always destined to be. As a leader, you need to be willing to find the Aslans in your life who have the insight and tools to help you break down the barriers to your leadership growth. It is up to you to submit to the process of refinement that will take you to the next level.

NOW GO LEAD

FIVE MINUTE REFLECTION

Have I been holding on to any hurts or resentments from my leadership journey that are manifesting themselves visibly in my actions? What are they?
What obvious "dragon scales" am I allowing to remain because I am unwilling to undergo the painful process of extraction?

FINALS AND FOREVERS

What is calling you?

As children, we see the passage of time as something we desperately want to accelerate. As adults, we just want it to slow down. It's such a tragedy we experience life this way. While the passage of time (relatively speaking) does not change, it is clear something in our brains tells us it does. I have very fond memories of growing up in the 80s and 90s. Every time I hear "Endless Summer Nights," it takes me back to a place where life was simple and slow. But it wasn't the decade that made the difference: it was and is my mindset. For whatever reason, we can look back and see things so clearly, but we are somehow unequipped to put any perspective on the reality of our current moment.

There are certain things in life we want to end. We want them to end so we can move on to the next thing, like a too-long meeting or a too-long doctor's appointment. We long to be free from bad relationships. We want the miserable and uncomfortable circumstances to be over. For any person, there is a list of things we would rather not continue to devote time and resources toward. Yet there is an undeniable part of our hearts that seeks eternity. It's built into our DNA at some level. You experience it when you are having a great and meaningful conversation with a friend, when you spend time with someone who makes you feel special, like no one else in the world, when you hold your child for the first time. We don't want life to be over, per se; we just want a life without any of the problems. If we could have a problem-free life, we could go on forever.

What does this all mean for leadership? Leaders have been blessed (and cursed) with the burden of a vision. To the leader, the vision represents the life they want someday. They see a world where the pursuit of their vision could become reality, and they spend the best of their years and the best of their resources in a quest to accomplish that goal. We laud this as a noble endeavor, and why not? The masses of the world stand to benefit the most when a leader succeeds in a worthy cause. We want people to be leaders who will sacrifice their lives for a vision we would otherwise never pursue. Yet, the life of the leader matters. Since I am writing this to you as the leader, I want to let you in on a little secret: ***Most leaders spend their entire lives without knowing that the destination is not actually where they will find the fulfillment they are pursuing.***

I can't even tell you how much I wanted high school to be over, and I was desperately ready to finish college. I put myself through back-to-back semesters with 20-hour class loads just so I could graduate without taking summer school. As I've mentioned before, I was aware of my leadership tendencies in my late teens, so I was always running ahead in life to advance my vision. I've been following the mantra of the Beach Boys going to Kokomo: "We'll get there fast, and then we'll take it slow." I remember having intentional conversations with my wife about retirement during my first year of work in Detroit. She was incredulous for me to be talking about the next phase of life when things were just getting started on the longest leg of the journey. I'm not alone. Most leaders (and Americans to some extent) are so wrapped up in trying to "get there", they are forgetting to experience what are truly the best years of their lives.

A leader's greatest gift to the world is the lives they impact along the journey to the vision. If you treat your organization, friends, and family merely as stepping stones on your ascent to greatness, you eventually will find yourself at a desolate pinnacle with only a view of the destruction and lost opportunities to fill your gaze. Today, resolve to embrace the journey and make the most of the time you have been given rather than wishing it away. Forever is a long time to go alone on the journey.

NOW GO LEAD

FIVE MINUTE REFLECTION

Is the pursuit of the vision causing me to miss the joy of the journey?
What am I sacrificing right now—something I can't get back and
may one day regret?

LEAVING

Can you just walk away?

The leadership journey is about moving forward. By very nature, moving forward means leaving something behind. That sounds easy enough right? Yet, the leadership journey is largely metaphysical, meaning progress follows a path fraught with emotional pitfalls, failures, and regrets. Any one of these can become an impassable roadblock, but for the leader, we must continually contend with the worst life throws at us and keep moving forward.

In 2010, I relocated my family to Oklahoma to start a new office for our growing engineering firm. This was a significant step for our company and an important milestone in my personal leadership journey. This would be my first time starting something new without the day-to-day companionship of my business partner. I remember well those lonely early days, sitting in an unoccupied office, staring out over the downtown Tulsa landscape. However, I was determined to succeed, and in about five years, we had a bustling team of sixteen people who I considered as close as family in so many ways. Back at the home office in Arkansas, however, things were starting to unravel.

We had traveled back to Arkansas for the Thanksgiving Holiday, and I managed to sneak out one evening to grab coffee with my business partner. He was stressed and starting to show signs of wear. The office in Arkansas had been such a huge supporter of the start-up effort in Oklahoma, but our company now had nearly 50 employees, and it was evident we needed stronger leadership at the home office to save our business and the people who were feeling the effects of our strained management. We decided that night, I would move back to Arkansas. Leadership was calling.

I've had plenty of difficult conversations during my time in leadership. Telling my team in Tulsa I was moving back to Arkansas was one of the most difficult messages I've ever had to deliver. It was hard for them, and I knew there would be some big shoes to fill in my absence. At the time, we really didn't have much of the video conferencing technology that exists today, so I knew there would be weeks and months when I wouldn't be able to see my friends, and indeed, the intimacy of the relationships would begin to fade as well. I spent a considerable amount of time mourning the loss and closing this chapter of my life.

It wasn't too long after we had moved back to Arkansas that a man named Benjamin William Hastings wrote a powerful song called "So will I." It is easily one of the seminal Christian worship songs of this century, and I was deeply impacted by it. It was during a season of mourning one day when I printed out a phrase from the lyrics of that song, and it has been taped to my keyboard at work ever since: *"if you left the grave behind you so will I..."*[1] As a leader, you will experience death along the journey. These words have been a steady and constant reminder to me of how the true leader must leave death behind to move forward. Sometimes it is the death of a relationship, sometimes it is the death of a dream, sometimes everything you hold dear will be taken from you. If you, as the leader, cannot free yourself to move forward from the grave, the whole organization will die with you.

Leader, this is a tough one. I know this because I have mourned some very difficult losses during my journey. I have told you many times: leadership is not for the weak and faint of heart. It may feel callous and cold to walk away from the death that will be part of your journey, but the pursuit of vision must continue. You have to be the one who leads the way through death and into the new life waiting on the other side.

NOW GO LEAD

---

1   Houston, J., Hastings, B. W., & Fatkin, M. (2017). So will I (100 billion X) [Song]. Hillsong Music Publishing

<u>FIVE MINUTE REFLECTION</u>

What are some deaths in my past I am having trouble leaving behind?

How has my leadership been hindered or stunted because of my unwillingness to move past the death of a relationship or dream?

WORTHY

Has it been worth it?

The idea of a calling on a person's life stirs an incredible amount of emotion in my heart. I am not easily convinced of many things, but I believe with all my heart that leadership is my life's calling. I've known this since I was a teenager. It took me some time to learn that knowing one's calling in life is a bit of a rarity in modern culture. However, if you take some time to look back on any success story, you will find an individual who found their calling and then spent the rest of their life pursuing the journey to fulfill it. I think some obvious questions arise here: does everyone have a true calling in life? How do I find my calling? Can I get through life without a calling?

Paul was a guy whose early life was dictated mainly by his circumstances rather than a true calling. He was born into a fiercely religious family and was sent off at a young age to learn his faith from the priesthood in Jerusalem. By the time he was grown, Paul had become one of the bright young leaders of his faith and was set up to pursue a career as a teacher of the law. Even under the rule of the Romans, Paul's position in the Jewish community provided him much latitude to exercise his own form of persecution against heretics and false teachers. In fact, at one point, Paul felt his entire calling in life was to act on behalf of God to purify the Jewish Nation by eradicating a newly formed offshoot of Judaism called "The Way." But this would not be Paul's destiny.

One day, Paul was out on a road trip to persecute some followers of The Way. As he was walking along the road, God revealed himself in the skies and told him everything he was doing was wrong. Instead of killing followers of The Way, he was now supposed to become a follower, and even further, become the voice of The Way to the entire Roman Empire. Paul's life changed in a moment, but for the first time, he had a true calling. It shattered the meaning he'd attached to everything he thought he'd accomplished up to that moment, but it also gave him an unflinching clarity about who he was becoming and what his life would require from that point forward.

Paul would later write to new followers of The Way how they should live a life worthy of the calling they have received. I imagine he wrote this with pangs of regret for things he did before he received his calling, but also with a burning heart for them not to waste a moment to pursue the journey with fervor. Leader, you have been called to something greater than most. Now I urge **you** to live a life worthy of that calling and pursue the vision with every breath you have been given.

NOW GO LEAD

<u>FIVE MINUTE REFLECTION</u>

Does leadership have a calling on my life, or have I found myself
simply leading because of my circumstances?
Do I need to find my calling and align my leadership with the
journey laid out before me?

THE ONSET

Are you brave enough to take the first step alone?

A leader in training will often spend years developing their vision before they take the first step on the journey. This is a critical time for the would-be leader, as they begin to develop their ideas about the world and how they will respond one day with their vision for the future. The unknown, and perhaps frightening part of this stage, is how the would-be leader has no idea whether even a single person will ever join them on the journey ahead. In so many ways, the hopes and dreams of one person and perhaps one day millions of people all exist in a singular idea of what will one day become the vision. As the aspiring leader, can you have the confidence to embark on the journey based solely on the vision?

Jesus spent thirty years in relative obscurity before embarking on his own journey. We get brief glimpses into the early parts of his life at birth and later at age twelve. Beyond that, there is nothing mentioned about the day-to-day happenings in his life. These were the years of grinding out hours at a regular job, learning and experiencing the challenges of dealing with difficult people, and of course, developing his vision for the world. This example really stands out from the way we pursue leadership today.

First, we need to understand it takes time for us to make the necessary preparations to lead. There is so much critical development happening in the heart and mind of a would-be leader right up through their 20s. Yet, we have a cultural mindset of once we graduate from college, we are automatically ready for the highest levels of leadership. I see it very often when a man or woman comes to me and says they are ready to lead but truly have no vision to pursue. They are unwilling to put in the time required to develop a vision and instead end up spending an entire decade trying to find a shortcut to get past the "years of obscurity" requirement essential to the process of preparing for the journey. Some might try going back to school for more advanced degrees or, more commonly today, moving from job to job every 12 months in an attempt to skip a few steps. The would-be leader must commit to the process.

Secondly, we need to take the time to develop the vision before presuming to lead anyone anywhere. If we are honest, it seems a little foolish to load up an entire busload of people and start driving them somewhere without any idea where you are going or why. Yet again, we get this backwards. We want the followers before we get the vision. In this pursuit, the would-be leader will rally hard to gain followers through any method possible. They believe (falsely) that once they get the followers, they can work out the vision along the journey. What they don't understand is the tasks and responsibilities of managing a group of people will preclude them from ever fully developing the vision. Instead, you end up with a wandering organization that never really grows or achieves anything significant. This organization will drift into oblivion over time, and the leader will fade with it.

There is another interesting narrative at the onset of Jesus's ministry. He is introduced to the world quite publicly by the leading prophet of the time. Instead of immediately taking a step towards the crowds, Jesus heads off alone for a final period of time to test his resolve. It is during this "final exam" his heart and vision are put to the test. **This is the first true step on the journey, and he takes it alone.** He understood something a true leader must understand as well: the vision must be refined and worthy; whether or not you ever gain a single follower, the journey must be worth your life.

Later, Jesus used a parable to describe his vision for the world. He described a wealthy man who decided to throw a grand and lavish party. He invited all the people he knew, and none of them showed up. So instead, he instructed his servants to go and bring in any person off the street who wanted to come to the party. The party was ultimately enjoyed not by the people who should've been there (the intended audience), but by people who wanted to be a part of the vision.

If the would-be leader can commit to the process and develop the vision, they are ready to begin the journey. Take the first step alone and don't think too much about who will end up joining you along the way. The truth is, the people you think should follow you probably won't, and there is an unknown world hungry to join you in the pursuit of the vision. Just trust your heart, and the vision will guide you.

NOW GO LEAD

<u>FIVE MINUTE REFLECTION</u>

Am I trying to lead without a vision?
Am I trying to skip some critical phases of development?
Do I need to slow down, commit to the process, and develop the vision?

THE BIGS

Are you worn out already?

Being a young leader is tough. Being a young leader who thinks they have it all figured out makes it even worse. Humility is such an important skill to develop early in the journey. Without it, your ambitions become selfish, and you begin to see the world as the enemy rather than the challenge you must rise to meet. Tim McGraw said it well, "I know you got mountains to climb, but always stay humble and kind..."

Jeremiah was called to leadership at a young age. From all accounts, it was his destiny to be a voice of truth to the world around him. So much so, that later in life God told Jeremiah "...before you were born, I set you apart..." However, having a destiny and a clear vision did not preclude Jeremiah from experiencing some of the pitfalls common to leaders along the journey. On one occasion, Jeremiah hit a bit of a rough patch. He had been working hard and doing all the right things; however, he just seemed to not be making any progress.

The people whose lives he was trying to influence were a bunch of obstinate blockheads who wouldn't listen to a word he said and thought they were doing just fine without his interference in their lives. In a moment of frustration, he cries out to God and asks to have them all killed off. Basically, Jeremiah was done. Done with leadership. Done with the journey. Done with the vision. The response Jeremiah hears back from God is a strong admonishment for leaders today. "*So, if you're worn out in this footrace with men, what makes you think you can race against horses?*" Let's unpack this.

First, there is the significance of Jeremiah's immaturity and inability to see beyond his current circumstances. Sometimes, as young leaders, we see our problems as too big and our skills too small. The world seems unfair because everyone and everything around us seems to be trying to derail us from reaching the vision. But it's important to remember, what you are facing today as a leader will one day seem small in comparison to what lies ahead. The leader must learn quickly to put seemingly insurmountable challenges into a manageable perspective. Is it okay to complain occasionally? Of course. It is also possible for a leader to develop a martyr syndrome they can never recover from. These leaders exit the journey early and say, "If only everyone else in the world weren't against me, I could've been the best leader the world has ever seen!"

Another thing to notice here is how God indicates there are much bigger things in store for Jeremiah in the future. When I started my firm at age 29, I was in awe of the successful businesses around me. I couldn't fathom what it would be like to have ten people working for me. I couldn't imagine ever having a million dollars in annual revenue. All of it just seemed so far out of reach, and the daily stuff I was dealing with seemed so trivial in light of the vision I was pursuing. Now I can look back and understand how every battle was simply a warm-up for the big race with the horses.

I should note how Jeremiah's journey got much more difficult. His career spanned almost five decades and was marked with heartache and persecution. No, the journey wasn't easy, but Jeremiah survived and eventually was vindicated when the message of his career was made manifest. Remember: every phase of the journey is preparing you for the next. Don't get discouraged and get lost complaining about the difficulty. This is the path of the leader; this is the path to the vision.

NOW GO LEAD

<u>FIVE MINUTE REFLECTION</u>

Am I complaining too much about the difficulty of my journey when I should instead develop a perspective to keep my eyes on the vision? Am I letting my current circumstances push me off track, or am I letting them prepare me for the greater journey ahead?
How can I use those circumstances to prepare me for the greater journey ahead?

TOO GOOD?

Can you have the life you want?

If I look at much of my writing on leadership, I can see that much of it revolves around difficulties, challenges, and sacrifice. What I don't think I have mentioned often enough, though, is that for any leader, **doing what you were born to do is absolutely the most rewarding thing in the world.**

Are there things you do as the leader no one else wants to do? Yes.

But these things are often what bring you the greatest joy in life in leadership. Along the same vein, a leader or would-be leader who never gets the opportunity to lead, or who never allows themselves to risk it, will find they live the plurality of their life building a pale reflection of the true calling of their heart. Today I want to invite you to the life you sometimes think is too good to be true. You can have it if you are willing to risk it all on a chance to lead from the truth of your heart.

I remember the first time I was given a group of people to manage. My first real "test," if you will. I quickly learned confidence in leadership is essentially a grand production in the beginning. Meaning you are expected to know what you are doing, but in reality, you start each day trying to figure out how to apply theory to practical application. Even so, some leadership tasks will come more easily than others. There will be moments to keep you smiling for days when you finally get through to someone or have a significant win along the journey.

Those stretches when your heart is free to lead. The road ahead is full of nothing but your dreams. It is a special place in the leadership journey, and I hope with all my heart you are willing to take a chance and pursue it. However, if it is such a great opportunity to pursue, what are the things keeping us back from embarking on the journey?

Fear and self-doubt are certainly at the top of the list of reasons not to pursue the vision. Too many people want to have the entire journey mapped out before they take the first step. I'm not saying planning isn't a good idea, but it will only take you so far.

Sometimes we doubt whether we have what it takes (the guts, the moxie) to leave our comforts behind and go boldly into the unknown. If you are experiencing these feelings, let me remind you it's common to many of the greatest leaders our world has ever known. When God called Moses to his first leadership assignment, he had nothing but excuses:

"Who am I that I should go...?"

"What if they do not believe me or listen to me...?"

"I am slow of speech and tongue."

"Please send someone else."

I'd like to sit here and make fun of this guy, but if I'm being honest, these same exact questions have been my own at some time or another. It is sad for me to watch a person with so much potential never answer the powerful call of leadership and instead offer up all the reasonable excuses to stay on the sidelines of life.

I hope you've been inspired to consider your own journey. This moment and this life will happen only once in all of time and space, never to return. Will you look back with wistful regret about what might have been, or will you have the courage to move in the now? Today, I encourage you to pursue your dream and answer the call to the life you were made to live.

NOW GO LEAD

FIVE MINUTE REFLECTION

Am I making excuses for not embarking on my own
leadership journey?
Have I let self-doubt and fear keep me from the life I've always
wanted to pursue?

PHOBIAS

Do you have fears?

Have you ever met someone who seemed fearless? Someone who could march right into an auditorium wearing nothing but a pair of socks and deliver an impassioned speech without batting an eye? Someone who never seems to back down from anyone, someone who runs toward trouble instead of hiding and avoiding problems? These people always seem to have it together, and the rest of us sit by and wonder why we can't be like that. Leaders are expected to be fearless and true paragons of might, grit, and steely resolve. We look to leaders in times of crisis. We want to be led out of danger and have someone hold our hand and protect us. *But is it ok for the leader to be afraid?*

A little secret about me: *I hate being afraid.* I also hate it when other people are living in fear. I hate when people have fears I don't understand, and I hate how those fears ruin their lives. Fear is a natural human response when we believe something bad is going to happen to us. The list of things we are afraid of ranges from common acrophobia to the more bizarre Alexinomia (look it up). Yes, fear is common, and we must be careful in today's culture not to minimize or trivialize another person's fears. And yet, the fears seem to be growing out of control, and we keep adding to the long list of reasons we never take risks in our lives or remain in shallow pools of complacency. We mistakenly believe the only way to move forward is to eliminate our fears, but the reality is the leader must choose to move forward with fear right beside them.

Whether you are out leading or sitting on the sidelines, you may have some real fears holding you back. I just want to let you know

I've been there. I know what it's like not to want to get out of bed in the morning because you know what the day has in store. It could be an uncomfortable talk with the bank, it could be ending an important relationship, or it could be simply standing in a room while you are castigated for a problem which developed under your watch. Fear in leadership can be paralyzing. **It's ok to be afraid, but the true leader must learn to manage fear and bring it under control, just like any other emotion common to the journey.** Sounds simple, right?

There's been more written about fear by people way smarter than me, so I won't try to say anything too profound here. However, I have found that, like so many other things in life, people have been dealing with fears for a really long time. If you follow the Biblical account, the first recorded words from Adam's mouth were "*I was afraid...*" Yes, our enemy, Fear, has been around from the dawn of human civilization, and he is not planning to leave us anytime soon. As leaders, we can either get up and battle fear each day or let it consume our lives and derail the pursuit of the vision.

In his book *Brave Companions* (read it!), David McCullough masterfully captures the stories and narratives of the men and women of history who were brave enough to look fear in the eye and dare to lead into the unknown. The stories are wide and varied but share a common theme: **It doesn't always take an accomplished hero to go out and change the world; it simply takes a leader who is willing to go on the journey in the face of fear and live in pursuit of the vision.**

NOW GO LEAD

FIVE MINUTE REFLECTION

Have I let a specific fear prevent me from making progress on the journey?
Have I taken myself out of the game for fear of losing or being responsible for others' suffering?
What will happen to my organization if fear wins?

FEELINGS

Should emotions inform or guide?

Ah emotions. Wonderful gifts, immensely gratifying, yet painfully persistent, distracting, and powerful enough to take control of our lives. We can all agree that without emotions, the journey would be unfulfilling and perhaps without purpose. Yet there are many moments along the way when emotions bring us down so low we just don't want to keep going. Whatever we may believe about the vision that led us to set out on our journey can be reduced to complete irrelevance in a moment of weakness, when we let our emotions overwhelm our normally balanced leadership. Why do we measure our leadership by how we feel after the last meeting instead of by what we consistently do?

I remember the first time I got fired by a client (yeah, it happens). Our original contract covered two projects, and the first was a bit of an onerous task. We were a little out of our depth, not from a technical standpoint, but certainly our lack of bandwidth nearly killed us. I was proud of our team for the way we persevered and didn't run away from the challenge. However, a few weeks after we made our final deliverable, the client brought me in for a "difficult discussion." Basically, they had lost confidence in our ability to deliver in the next phase of work and wanted to move on to another consultant. It was a crushing moment and something I had not experienced yet in my career. I remember driving home, considering myself a complete failure, and I let the voices in my head take over for a moment. I also knew I would have to deliver the news to my team the next day and somehow convince them things would be okay despite the setback. These are the moments when having a business partner can be invaluable. I called my partner to share the news, and with his steady words of encouragement, he reminded me of the bigger picture and got me back on track.

On the leadership journey, we set out to pursue a vision, and along the journey, we are guided by our beliefs. As leaders, we can get off course when we confuse emotions with beliefs or lose the ability to discern between the two. But we must remember: belief is not a feeling; it is an act of will. There will be challenges and difficulties in your journey, and some will hurt emotionally. In those moments, it is natural to examine the source of the pain and decide whether returning to a vulnerable position makes sense - especially with another emotional haymaker on the table.

I have found, even for the strongest leaders, it is essential to surround yourself with constant reminders of your beliefs. A strong belief in the vision will anchor your soul amid the emotional hurricanes you encounter along the path. In ancient times, it was common practice to write words of dogma on the doorpost of your home and wear reminders of your belief on your wrist. I believe we still need to continue this practice in modern culture. For myself, I keep printed reminders of the vision I am pursuing just beneath my computer, where I spend most of my days.

Feelings are good things, but we can't let them distort our view of our belief in the vision. The leader must guide with a steady hand and let reality serve as the litmus test for success on the path. Be intentional about setting up the constant reminders you need to anchor your soul in the belief in the vision. When you are well anchored, you will gain the strength to make progress in your pursuit, even through the toughest emotional storms of the journey.

NOW GO LEAD

FIVE MINUTE REFLECTION

Have I let temporary emotions pull me away from my belief in the vision?

Do I have the clarity right now to know the vision is worth pursuing, even during the hardest stretches of the journey?

COSMETICS

What are you fixing?

In early 2022, Americans spent roughly $15 billion on cosmetic procedures, with the majority of that amount going toward elective invasive surgery. Fifteen billion dollars could buy 7,500 miles of new roads or cover four-year college degrees for nearly 400,000 students. Numbers like these show how much priority we give to physical appearance. We drive away from our $450 Botox treatment and complain about crappy roads, and it's just too expensive to send our kids to college. We'd often "rather fix (our) makeup than try to fix what's going on."

The leader must not be swept up in the trend of simply looking good at the expense of not addressing the most important problems, which are often easy to ignore. When you go into a meeting with your team, they will all look to you as the leader to set the tone. Will you address the uncomfortable issues of the day or simply put more lipstick on the pig and try to make it another week, hoping the issues will go away without some uncomfortable or unpleasant conversations.

In his time, Jesus took a tough stance against this approach to leadership. Calling them "hypocrites," he put the leaders of his day on blast in a very public display. "*...you have neglected the most important things...you clean the outside of the cup and dish, but inside you are filthy...*" His admonishment was not so much about whether appearances mattered, but rather how they cared much more about what people thought of them, and whether they had the integrity to match their polished façade.

The true leader cannot ignore the unappealing realities in their personal life and the life of the organization. Doing so only perpetuates the façade which will collapse when the corrosion from the inside eventually finds its way to the surface. Commit today to humble yourself and acknowledge what needs to be addressed and gain the freedom to lead with confidence that comes from alignment of heart and image.

NOW GO LEAD

FIVE MINUTE REFLECTION

What example am I setting in my organization when it comes to prioritizing integrity over appearance?
Am I continually ignoring a persistent personal or organizational issue because it might mean exposing and acknowledging an uncomfortable truth that is eroding my leadership from the inside?

ON THE EDGE

Can you let go of the past?

Our senses help us understand our place in the world. What we see, smell, touch, and hear at any given moment shapes our current definition of reality. Yet there exists an undefined, etheric longing inside of all of us for something beyond our perceived reality. For many people, the battle between reality and the pursuit of fulfillment is a lifelong struggle to let go of what makes sense and take a risk to find the one thing capable of making all the difference. I am reminded of a song from my past, "On the edge of all I need, Still I cling to what I see."

When the Israelites left Egypt, God told them to move into the land he had promised them. It wasn't too long after the Exodus when the nation reached the edge of this promise. Moses dispatched a team of scouts to check out the fortifications, and they came back with their report:

"We went into the land to which you sent us, and it does flow with milk and honey! Here is its fruit. But the people who live there are very powerful, and the cities are fortified and very large."

The people were quite disheartened by the report and decided against moving to occupy the land they had been promised. This, of course, led to forty years of wandering in the desert for the new nation. By the time they were given another chance to take the land, everyone from the first generation of the nation had died.

This story fills me with sadness, anger, and regret. It is such a powerful reminder of how short life is. You may not get more than one great opportunity to take hold of the life you were meant to live. Often the greatest opportunities in life require letting go of what makes sense and moving forward with nothing but faith. It may be a faith that flies in the face of common sense, but it is undoubtedly a faith destined to grow your leadership.

There may be some days when it feel like all we are doing is walking by faith. It may feel like a dangerous road, but the true leader must learn to incorporate faith into the everyday reality created by the sight and sound of the journey. Today, commit to moving past the edge of only what you can see and into places where only the bravest dare set foot.

NOW GO LEAD

FIVE MINUTE REFLECTION

What are the critical opportunities I have missed with long-term consequences for my future?
Where am I holding myself back because I am unwilling to make a decision I know will require faith in the face of reality?

THE WISDOM

Do you have what it takes to lead?

Earlier I wrote about a seminal trip to Vermont to renew my spirit and find a fresh vision for the future. Certainly, I feel like I had the right motivations and was seeking the right things on the trip. Still, an important truth became evident to me during the retreat. What I wanted to gain and learn was not waiting for me in a remote little cabin by the lake; it was already with me, long before I made the first mile of the journey.

Today, it's popular in our culture to "go find ourselves." We spend tons of money traveling around the world, hoping to find the experience that will be life-changing. We find ourselves moving into a new home, whether across town or across the country, hoping to escape our circumstances and gain a fresh start in life. Yet most often, we settle into our new environments and within a few short weeks or months, realize nothing meaningful has really changed. At some point, we are all faced with the reality - real change in our lives starts in the heart, soul, and mind.

There is a well-known story of a son who was raised by a father who taught him the difference between right and wrong and how to live a respectable life. However, when the son was old enough to leave home, he took all the money his father had set aside for him and decided to experience all life had to offer. For a moment it was exhilarating, but eventually the money ran out, and he found himself homeless and starving. In his desperation, clarity hit - living with his father no longer seemed so bad after all.

He crawled back to his father, hoping against hope for a second chance. What he received instead was the open arms of love and forgiveness. The son, just like many of us, believed there was something new and exciting to be gained out in the world. What he found instead was disappointment and failure. But what stayed with him were the memories and lessons learned in the daily work on his father's farm.

As a leader, you will be tempted at times to take all your chips off the table and walk away from the journey. This temptation often comes during the challenging and maybe even the mundane seasons of life. We hope to go somewhere else to find the answers, but in our hearts, we know challenges and occasional boredom are waiting for us no matter where we go.

The true leader must stay the course until its very end. The temptation to take another path or cash out early will always be lurking. I want to encourage you today to strengthen your resolve. These moments of crisis will pass, and the team you are leading will continue to need your unwavering pursuit of the vision.

NOW GO LEAD

FIVE MINUTE REFLECTION

Have I let my thoughts deceive me into thinking the leadership journey would be easier if I were on another path?
What selfish desires are clouding the vision of my leadership path?

LASTING CHANGE

What are the chains of my past?

The quiet lull of the first week of the new year always gives me the opportunity to spend some time looking back over the past year. Recently, a couple of people close to me have casually mentioned noticing a marked change in my leadership. I started thinking about whether this alleged change was real and, if so, why it happened. My reflection led me to the conclusion - indeed, I am not the same person I was a year ago. Moreover, there are specific, evident actions which led to this change, and, most importantly, they are essential to personal growth on the leadership journey.

Before I get there, I need you to get in your own head for a minute. Think about times of crisis in your life. You've probably had some in the past 18 months; maybe you are in one right now. These are the moments when life hits you hard. They make you question all your decisions. They put you in a panic mode, and you are suddenly ready to make any and every decision necessary to find relief. We make vows to God, ourselves, and others, like "I will never let this happen again," or, "If I make it out of this, I promise to make some real changes."

You know what I'm talking about. Sadly, in my experience I've noticed most people who come out of crisis slowly fade back into routine and are lulled back into normalcy by the steady passage of each new sleep cycle. Deep down, we know when we are doing this that we are headed towards the inevitable return of the crisis, yet we just can't face the truth of a different outcome which would mean facing big and often painful decisions.

The book of Judges, in the Old Testament of the Bible, chronicles the early history of the Hebrews as they were given their first taste of freedom as a new nation. In very short order, they made some bad decisions and got themselves into trouble. Repeatedly, they would cry out to God, who would rescue them, and things would be good for a while, only to inevitably fall back into bad decision-making and end up with another crisis on their hands.

If you read the narrative, it really is a story of absurdity. If you have a few minutes, take a look at how many times the phrase: "*Yet again the People of Israel went back...*" is repeated. It leaves you screaming in frustration at these idiots who can't learn a simple lesson. I find it interesting when God talks about his people during these times, He doesn't call them idiots, rather he refers to them as "stiff-necked." That phrase for stubbornness is actually a reference to an ox or plow-horse that refuses to take direction from their master. Quite interesting when you consider that imagery.

So, what did I learn this year? I have shared in my writings the details and emotions emerging as I worked through the pain of being broken and rebuilt. Looking back, a few key actions rose above the rest and led me to success.

1. I Didn't Run Away.

Fleeing from discomfort, pain, or problems is a natural reaction to a bad situation, and people do it all the time. However, when you run away from your circumstances, you also hope to avoid dealing with the personal accountability that led to the crisis. This will never lead to real growth.

2. I Committed to Face Myself and My Mistakes.

Looking in the mirror and acknowledging who we are in a moment of crisis is so humiliating. But it is absolutely the path forward. It takes getting comfortable with the truth before we can break down the walls holding us back.

3. I Refused to Go Back.

I fought hard against the urge to retreat daily for almost three straight months this past year during a particularly challenging period of the journey. The calm fields of normalcy were so attractive, especially when so many raw wounds were being opened each day during the healing process.

4. I Embraced the Pain of Brokenness.

It is a very natural reaction to want to avoid pain. It's probably the main reason people quit growing as they get older. When you're an adult, no one is going to force you to endure pain. However, the true leader understands how brokenness is a necessary step towards healing.

5. I Quit Worrying About What Other People Think.

When too much of your life and self-esteem is built on the opinions of others, change can be almost impossible. It leads to common non-starters, such as a fear of failure and shame. As long as you are worrying about the thoughts and opinions of others over your own well-being, it will be nearly impossible to move forward with the things requiring change in your life.

6. I Yielded Control of the Outcome.

When you choose to embrace the process of brokenness, the immediate response is to want a hand in the rebuilding process. It helps to remember: doing things your own way played a big role in bringing you to the crisis. The better choice is to let yourself be guided by someone wiser than you and accept the outcome that naturally (or supernaturally) develops.

Here is what I want to leave you with: stop making excuses. Break out of the chains of fear and normalcy this next year. You have one chance and one life to live. Do not let the sum of your life disappear into the obscurity of routine. Choose courage. Break free, and pursue a life unbound by chains of your own making. Freedom is calling.

NOW GO LEAD

<u>FIVE MINUTE REFLECTION</u>

Is there a very obvious situation you have avoided facing?
Have you chosen the open fields of old routines over the hard work of leadership?
What are your learning in your leadership journey that will help carry you through the next year and embrace change?

GET OUT OF JAIL

Are you a willing prisoner?

Today is the first day of the rest of your life. I know what you're thinking, but this is not just some trite cliché you should quickly dismiss. Almost every culture in our world celebrates the passing of time with the birth of a new year. It is a humble reminder - time keeps marching on, but it is also an opportunity to leave the past behind for the hopes of a better future. The decisions we make today determine the quality of life we will have tomorrow. It takes wisdom to understand that everything we have today is the result of a small decision made in the past. Here's the thing about decisions: we often don't know if they were good or bad until we see the outcome - sometimes years later. Decisions that are easy to make in a moment can create prisons for our future or form foundations for unlimited growth. So, what are you planning right now? Do you want to make the best out of your prison sentence, or do you want to break out and start building the future you've been longing for?

Many will remember "The Shawshank Redemption" as the story of an innocent man spending years in prison and eventually finding a way to escape. However, an interesting side narrative develops throughout the movie about the various prisoners who are paroled and placed in a work-release program to help them adjust to life on the outside. While behind bars, all of the prisoners want their freedom, but as the movie unfolds almost everyone who makes it into the work release program either finds a way to go back to prison or decides to commit suicide. They've been in prison so long they no longer know how to handle true freedom and succeed in a world without the confines of constant oversight and thirty-foot concrete walls.

For many of us, it seems absurd for anyone to prefer prison or death over freedom, but hold up for a second and take a look in the mirror. Have you ever made decisions in the past which ultimately created a prison for your future? Is it financial? A relationship? Maybe it's an addiction to food, sex, or social media. Whatever the case, you've become so accustomed to your situation you have lost all sense of true freedom. Instead, you have resigned your future to the pale gray walls of confinement defining the limits of your vision.

Leaders, as much as we would like to think otherwise, we are also not immune to our own prisons. A prison, in whatever form it takes, limits our vision and, therefore, limits our ability to lead. To the outside world, Andy Dufresne might have appeared to be confined, but the truth is, for him, the walls of the prison were not the limit of his vision. He worked consistently (for 19 years) to pursue his vision despite the daily difficulties he faced. As leaders, we must do the same.

The steps to freedom are often more difficult than we would like to think. The first step, of course, is acknowledging your prison and committing to freeing yourself. The second is being brave enough to live and grow in the open waters of freedom. A leader who is truly free can have a vision unbound by their own circumstances and open to possibilities that few dare to pursue.

NOW GO LEAD

FIVE MINUTE REFLECTION

What past decisions have created prisons that I now live in? Have I grown so accustomed to my circumstances I have let my vision shrink and my hope grow weak? What changes can I make to break free from the prison and cast a vision of freedom for those around me?

LIFE LOST

Have you made peace with the sacrifice?

"Where is the life we have lost in living?
Where is the wisdom we have lost in knowledge?
Where is the knowledge we have lost in information?"
T.S. Eliot

Eliot wrote these words during a time of great change, as the pace of life was starting to increase rapidly for the typical American. Although relevant at the time, I can't imagine he had any idea of what the pace of life might look like today. I had the privilege of growing up in rural America with a slow-paced life. However, I was thrust into a whole new world when I moved to Detroit in my early 20s. There is an energy that builds around the seemingly unbridled avarice of corporate America, and I was absolutely taken in by the newness of it all. Every time I would go back home to visit my family, I would pontificate about the great advantages of the pace of city life and lament the poor souls who had to live out their existence in the hundred-acre wood of yesterday's world.

But now I am firmly in the middle of my life, and I have started trying to put some perspective on the past 25 years. I wonder whether the choices I have made have led me to a better life, or perhaps if I have lost something along the way by "living" in the culture of my day. I can say unequivocally that some of the things that were important to me at 20 are not nearly as critical today. In the same way, when we think about the leadership journey, we have to pause and consider whether achieving the vision is worth the price of the journey.

In our modern culture, this manifests as a phenomenon called the fear of missing out (FOMO). FOMO is the idea that pursuing a singular vision means missing out on many opportunities available in life. If I commit to a career too soon, I might miss the chance to travel abroad, or if I choose to have children in my early 20s, I might miss the opportunity to enjoy the season of being young and married without kids. We have to realize that FOMO exists because our time to live is finite. It is true - we don't have time to do everything under the sun; **We have to choose.**

I am not immune to moments of waxing nostalgic or thinking about what could've been, but wisdom tells me the demand for a choice is what moves us forward along the journey. Without the decision to take the necessary steps on the journey, we will never attain the vision. Without the sacrifice of "what could've been," we will never know the greater joys of "what dreams may come."

I've said many times before that sacrifice is a critical, ongoing activity for the growing leader. The real "life lived" is the pursuit of a worthy vision. There will always be distractions trying to pull your attention and energy toward fleeting pleasures, but today is a reminder to turn your face resolutely toward the vision and proceed with boldness.

NOW GO LEAD

FIVE MINUTE REFLECTION

How has the fear of missing out distracted me from the pursuit of the vision?

What sacrifices have I made along the journey, and have I made peace with those choices?

JIM JONES AND THE BASS

How well do you own failure?

I hate the feeling of being ashamed. The feeling usually follows a moment of public failure or a forced acknowledgment of a personal shortcoming. As a leader, you will have moments when you come up short or fail spectacularly in front of your entire organization. How should the leader respond when everything in your heart and soul is telling you to hide and run away?

We've all had these moments; I might as well share mine. I was a precocious nine-year-old little boy, and my parents would take me to church every Sunday morning and evening. I usually did ok in the morning services, as the church had plenty of kid-friendly activities to keep us occupied. Sunday nights, however, were a totally different story. To this day, I believe I experienced some of the greatest boredom in my life during those hours. And of course, it was all compounded by the crushing reality of missing the Disney Sunday-night movie everyone would be talking about the next day at school.

While initially it was a requirement for me to sit right next to mom and dad, I eventually was granted the privilege to sit anywhere in the sanctuary if I behaved and stayed within eyeshot. This was a welcome reprieve that ultimately got me into a lot of trouble. Ironically, my favorite spot was usually the second pew near the piano. Brother Jim Jones would sit on the otherwise empty pew right in front of me and play bass guitar with his little amp while we all sang hymns. Once the music was over, he would go back and sit with his wife Rosie during the sermon and then make it back to the front for the invitation hymn at the end of every service.

One particular Sunday night, I was sitting alone in my pew during the sermon. For whatever reason, the minister began a rather lengthy prayer. So long in fact, that I eventually opened my eyes and started looking around. Every eye was closed but my own. Boredom took hold of me and I reached over the pew and started to fiddle with Brother Jim's bass guitar. I had never touched a guitar, so naturally I started turning all the knobs and levers, just messing around. Without knowing it, what I had actually done was loosen every string on the guitar and turn the volume on the pick-up from a three to a ten. As soon as the prayer was over, I sat back in my pew, and the sermon continued with no one the wiser...that is, until it was time for the invitation hymn.

As was normal, Brother Jim walked down and grabbed his bass while the minister wrapped up the sermon. The first few chords from "Just As I Am" rang serenely from the piano and organ. As soon as it was time for Jim to join in, the most sinful, evil, and horrendous sounds began to pour forth from the little Peavy amp under the pew. All eyes were immediately on Brother Jim, who by this time had gone rapidly from embarrassment to full-blown rage, and it was all focused on a scared little boy who was desperately praying for the Lord to return before the hymn ended. Outside of the impending fear of retribution, the only other emotion I distinctly remember was of how ashamed I was of what I had done.

When you screw up, it really sucks. You let people down, and you suddenly feel unworthy in your role as a leader. The leader, who is held to be a paragon of excellence, will occasionally be exposed to the fallibility common to all humanity. What do we do in these moments?

For starters, one of the most important things for a leader is to never take themselves too seriously. If you create or foster an image of your-self which is impossible to maintain or doesn't allow for an occasional slip, then you'll constantly feel the need to hide your faults from the people around you.

Secondly, it is important to remember how failure is common to everyone, and, in most cases, it does not diminish your ability to lead. You still have the goods; you just have to regain the confidence to keep leading.

Later that evening, after the "bass incident," I had to confront Jim and acknowledge what he already knew; that I had messed with his guitar. I wasn't able to look him in the eyes as I confessed, but I remember the relief I felt when he wrapped his arms around me and said, "It's ok, young man." It might have been the first real lesson I learned about leadership: *owning up to your failures is the first step towards recovery along the journey.*

NOW GO LEAD

FIVE MINUTE REFLECTION

Have I let a moment of shame or embarrassment derail my leadership?
Have I gone into hiding, or have I convinced myself my leadership is no longer effective because I've let my image become more important than pursuing the vision?

RISKY BUSINESS

Are you taking the right leadership risks?

As a leader, you sometimes must take risks. It is a necessary part of the journey, and your ability to know when to take the right risk at the right moment can make all the difference in the level of success you will see. If you are overly risk-averse, you'll rarely see the gains like those who are more comfortable taking some big swings now and again. Unfortunately, life is just too short to wait around for decades trying to gain success with an ultra-safe approach.

During the spring of my senior year of high school, I had been single for about 4-5 months (a true lifetime in the world of a high schooler). Fortunately, I had agreed to be the high school mascot for the basketball season, and I spent a lot of time with the cheer squad during practices, games, and bus rides. But, as far as potentially dating any of the cheerleaders, I didn't really have a lot of options. The girls I was interested in were in other relationships. There was a particular girl on the squad I really liked who was locked in a long-term relationship, but I had also heard the squad captain might be available.

For context, the way things worked in small town Oklahoma was **everyone** sent flowers and balloons to their sweetheart at school on Valentine's Day. All day long, the front office at the high school would call people out of class to go up front to pick up their deliveries. There were a couple of options for getting this done, but most folks went to Floral Fashions a few weeks ahead of time and put in their order. So, taking a gamble, I decided to send some roses (anonymously) to the captain of the cheer squad. And, because I was the bulldog mascot at the time, I decided to sign the card with a paw print (me trying to be clever).

Two days before Valentine's, I found out the captain of the squad had gotten a boyfriend from another school I was unaware of (not good). I also found out the girl I really liked had split with her long-time beau. The very next day, I ran over to Floral Fashions to talk to the florist. He told me that the truck was already loaded for delivery and my only option was to try to intercept the card after it was dropped off at the school. He gave me a blank envelope that I filled out with the new name, hoping to do a quick swap at school. That sounds easy in theory, but our high school secretary was a master of her own little fiefdom and did not suffer fools who would tread on her domain lightly.

The morning of February 14th arrived (I didn't sleep all night). I had band practice for the first hour off-site, so I was hoping against hope the flowers wouldn't be delivered before second period. After band class, I ran to the front of the high school and found the room where all the deliveries were being gathered. It was a veritable sea of mylar and baby's breath. Truly, every arrangement was indiscernible from the others. I snuck in, and I kid you not, before the door closed behind me, I heard the secretary yell out my name, "You can't go in there!" I was searching frantically for the envelope with the right name on it, and I finally found it. I got the card swapped out just as the secretary put her hand around my collar and pulled me out of the room.

I arrived late to second period, which ironically was a class I shared with both of the girls from the cheer squad. They were close friends and sat next to each other. Within just a few minutes, the announcement came across the overhead for the girl to come pick up her flowers. She came back to her desk and opened the card while all her friends gathered around. I had a prime view to watch it all unfold. She looked at the card, a little confused at first, and then it dawned on her that I might be her secret admirer. She looked straight at me and said, "Brandon, did you send this to me?" She was a pretty smart girl.

Of course, when I set all this in motion, I did not anticipate being called out in a roomful of my peers about whether I was the sender or not. Depending on my answer and her response, I could be facing serious ridicule. I had no time to think, so I just said "Yeah." The gaggle of teenage girls swarmed around her before I could see her expression in response. And of course, by then the teacher had called the class back to order. I spent the next 45 minutes in agony, waiting to know my fate. At the end of class, she walked up and handed me a note with her phone number on it. **Victory!**

It may seem like a trivial matter in retrospect to reach out to someone you like and share your feelings, but I can assure you - in the brain of the high-school version of me, I felt like I was putting everything on the line. Funny enough, I later learned it wasn't just dumb luck at play when I finally got the her phone number. The way I had carried myself as the school mascot in her presence in the weeks leading up to the moment told a much bigger story about who I was than a simple gesture of anonymity. The reality is, it's oftentimes the work you are putting in during the mundane hours which leads to success when you decide to take a big swing. Today is your invitation to take the big risk with courage and confidence. The hard work you are putting in day in and day out means your risks are actually likely to pay off more often than not.

NOW GO LEAD

FIVE MINUTE REFLECTION

Am I willing to take some big risks in the pursuit of the vision, or have I been too conservative in my approach and missed out on some big opportunities?
What is one big risk I might be willing to take on this year?

FREE SOLO

Can you go alone on this journey?

I got a message from my mom a couple of days ago about my dad needing to have an emergency quadruple bypass. The news was a little jarring, and as with most unexpected situations, I didn't have much time to react. In the hours leading up to the surgery, my thoughts settled on my dad and our relationship together. In many ways, my dad has given me a profound sense of place in the world as a son. I have taken on many other roles over the years as a husband and a father, but being a son has always given me great comfort.

It embodies the idea of being watched over, by someone who has my best interests at heart, with unconditional love. As I sit here, I realize, I haven't lived under the same roof with my parents for over 30 years. Yet, there has always been this quantum of solace in the back of my mind that, if everything in my life fell apart, I could always go back to my dad, and he would give me everything he could. So, when I considered the outcomes of this open-heart surgery, I was forced to reckon with a potential reality where he would no longer be with me, and it was a pretty sobering moment.

I didn't know much about rock climbing until I watched the 2018 documentary about Alex Honnold's attempt to climb El Capitan, one of the most famous rock formations in the world. Of course, this rock face had been conquered many times. But what was particularly interesting about Alex's story was that he wanted to make the climb "free solo," meaning he would attempt it without any traditional safety gear, such as ropes or climbing partners. In a free-solo climb, a single mistake would mean certain death, as there would be nothing to stop you from falling 3,000 ft to the bottom. After a couple of false starts, Honnold finally started up the rock face on June 3rd, 2017. It is truly a terrifying spectacle to behold as you watch the video. Even the camera workers couldn't help but look away at certain critical points along the ascent. Nevertheless, Alex stayed focused, and a mere four hours later, he emerged at the summit.

I've spoken many times about the loneliness that leaders experience. We may start our journey with a cadre of supporters, family, and friends, but the further we go along the journey, the safety net seems to dwindle away. Often, the final and most difficult stretches of the journey are made alone, without any guarantees of our safety. It can be a little unsettling in those moments when you realize you are moving into a new phase of the journey which, on one hand, is familiar. Yet you are now forced to operate for the first time without many of the comforts you've relied on for so many years.

Oftentimes, we can get too comfortable along the way. We can reach a point where we think we have nothing left to learn, or we assume we can always rely on the safety nets in our lives if things fall apart. However, the true leader understands we must be intentional about learning everything we can from those who have gone before us because the time we have with them is undoubtedly finite. Today, take time to reach out to the ones who have been a constant source of comfort to you and acknowledge how you wouldn't be the leader you are today without them.

NOW GO LEAD

FIVE MINUTE REFLECTION

How has my leadership been defined by the people who have
supported me along the way?
Is my leadership at a point where I can confidently move forward in
the journey if the comfort of my supporters were suddenly
taken away?

GPS

Where are you starting from?

For nearly 30 years now, and certainly for multiple generations of automobile drivers, we have had the modern advent of global positioning systems that give us access to turn-by-turn directions to any destination on the planet. We have mostly lost or forgotten the skills of using an atlas, or printing directions off the internet (MapQuest anyone?). We can simply grab our phones and ask for directions to anywhere and then we are given a happy blue line to follow to our desired destination. Have you ever thought for a minute how wonderful it would be if there was a GPS for the leadership journey? We may not have that technology today, but there is something critical to be learned about why GPS works and why our leadership journey can never start until we have one essential piece of information.

I remember well the early days of starting my business. There was a lot of controlled chaos, mostly fueled by fear and unbridled naivete. As is common with the growth of a business, the inevitable problems emerged that required skillful leadership to solve and move the organization forward. The problem was, we were running a little short on such individuals at the time, and it quickly dawned on me that I was the one who needed to start growing. The circumstances I found myself in, whether of my own creation or the forces around me, pushed me to consider that I must now figure out a path to grow my own leadership skills or risk the future of the entire organization.

As a visionary, I've always been pretty good at figuring out "the solve" or the "final picture" for a problem. But much like a GPS, you can have a firm idea of your destination, but if you can't determine where you are starting from, the GPS and your leadership are pretty useless tools. This led me to an important truth that I have had to revisit many times along the journey: **you can't plan a journey to success without first knowing where you are starting from.**

It actually is not an easy thing to understand where you are starting from in your leadership journey. Most certainly we are all in different places because no single leadership journey is the same. We may face many of the same obstacles, but the turns in the path and the length of the journey are all predicated on the location of the starting line. Being able to rise above your circumstances and gain enough perspective to know your current state is something many people cannot do, and honestly few leaders have the discipline to do it well.

Most of the time we decide we are going somewhere, content that we have a destination in mind, and start taking steps in one arbitrary direction after another. We have no idea what the journey is going to cost us because we have no idea whether we are 10 miles or 500 miles away. We hope we are going in the right direction, and occasionally we might look up at the sun to try and get our bearings, but eventually and inevitably we get lost or run out of gas, and we once again find ourselves in a place with no identity and no idea of the direction forward.

I've seen too many leaders and organizations get excited about the destination but ultimately fail to make any progress because they aren't willing to be honest about where they are in the present moment. Today is an encouragement to maintain a true self-awareness of where you are in the journey because without a place to start, you'll never know what it takes to reach the destination.

NOW GO LEAD

FIVE MINUTE REFLECTION

Have I set out on a journey without first taking a true measure of my starting position?

What provisions and preparations do I need to make before starting on the journey to ensure success?

CLOSING THOUGHTS

I don't know how long it has taken you to get here, but congratulations! Leading yourself is something few will ever learn how to do. But here you are, ready to take on the next phase of the journey: Leading Others. Yet even as you move forward, remember this journey is an additive process.

The burden will only become greater, and the path will narrow as we move forward. As you begin to take on the responsibility of leading others, you will soon be faced with the reality that you are the ceiling on others' ability to grow under your leadership. Therefore, you must continue leading and developing yourself if you ever hope to be successful leading others. This is only a pause, not an ending. I look forward to re-engaging with you as the journey continues.

Now Go Lead Vol. 2: Lead Others
Available Fall 2026

CLOSING BASELINE
LEADERSHIP ASSESSMENT

Rate each statement on a scale of 1 to 10, 1 being not true, 10 being very true.

1. I have made measurable progress towards my vision in the past year.

2. I know the things I need to be working on every day to make progress.

3. I am disciplined with my time and not letting daily distractions slow me down.

4. I am using hard metrics as a measure of my success instead of comparing myself to others.

5. I am honest with myself about my shortcomings and am leading with humility.

6. I am hyper-aware of the personal biases that intrude on my leadership abilities.

7. My closest relationships are healthy.

8. I am having 1-on-1 time with a mentor regularly.

9. I am mentoring at least 2-3 others in my organization regularly.

10. I am being open and vulnerable in my important relationships.

11. I have open channels for feedback from my team or organization.

12. I have a clear sense of who I am as a leader.